Managing With Respect

A Model for Success Based on Real World Experience

Strategies and Lessons for Managing People and Business Resources

By James P. DuBreuil

DEDICATION:

To the many wonderful women who have played such a significant role in
my life, and especially, in memory of Tricia.

Managing With Respect

Table of Contents

Acknowledgements

I have had the good fortune of knowing some very remarkable people in both my professional and personal life. And although I have carved my own somewhat disjointed path, navigating through career and family circumstances, their unwavering support, guidance and understanding has always provided a reliable safe haven even in the most difficult of times. *Managing With Respect* could not have been a reality without the intelligent efforts and substantive contributions of several people. These trusted advisors played no small role in influencing my perspective, outlook and even actions over the years. It was no accident that I asked them to read my manuscript and I know that I could have never realized the success and satisfaction I've enjoyed without these special family members, friends and colleagues. It is with the utmost love and respect for them that I present them to you.

My sister Eileen is a strong and independent woman, and one of the smartest people I know. Despite our close relationship, her objective review and suggestions of this work kept me on target and were invaluable in helping to produce a resource that would be meaningful and interesting to a wide audience. I cannot thank her enough for her time commitment and astute feedback.

Carol Folau just happens to be my cousin, but with more than 30 years in social services, she provided a perspective on the writings that was instrumental in confirming a reader appeal beyond the commercial business world. She also applied her

4

keen awareness of the written word to provide outstanding critique and valuable input to the text. Carol's extraordinary blend of pragmatism and compassion served the people of New York for many years, and I am grateful to her for providing such a unique and meaningful review.

Professor Earl Hill is a friend and colleague who has enjoyed two very successful careers. At IBM and now at Emory University, Earl exudes professionalism and a common sense approach to work, career and family. His review of the *Managing With Respect* manuscript provided me powerful and unique feedback that resulted in relevant edits and a better overall product. I am extremely appreciative to Earl for his input on the book and mentorship over the years.

A friend of more than two decades, Bill Papp has had a variety of experiences and possesses a unique intellect and thoughtful approach to life's complexities. His reading of my final proof allowed me to get one more objective assessment before making it available to the public. I am so very grateful for his ongoing friendship and time spent reviewing the book.

Above all, I am eternally indebted to my beautiful wife Sharon, the strongest person I've ever known. Her love, support and companionship have provided a foundation from which to create. Despite a lifetime filled with medical challenges and deep personal loss, Sharon has not only persevered but manages to bring out the best in me and others whose life she touches. I am blessed to be able to share my life with this remarkable woman. Her contributions to the writing of this book go well beyond proofreading and editing.

Preface

My journey of a work life began in the summer I turned 14 years old. My father and his business partner had agreed to not have family members work at their now well established automotive service station but I seem to remember my mother pleading with them to "get me out of the house!" Too young to legally operate the gas pumps, I followed my father around wiping windshields, pounding hubcaps on wheels and scrubbing the garage floor more often than I ever cleaned my own room at home.

Over time I learned a lot from my very first manager, my father, and it is no coincidence that more than forty years later, I still remember lessons he taught by virtue of his mild-mannered temperament and ability to treat all people with dignity and fairness. I once heard him fire a worker who was calling in sick one more time after being warned that if he did; it would be his last time. I knew my dad was disgusted that the call came but he simply told the employee, "Okay, you can come in Saturday to pick up your final pay." That was it. He walked out of the front office and returned with the "Help Wanted" sign for the window. When the terminated employee showed up Saturday there was no incident or hard feelings. There was no need to belabor the issue. The pay envelope and simple good bye was exchanged and it was over. I thought, "Is that how easy it is to fire someone?" Of course there was a lot more going on than my 14 year old brain could assimilate at that time but there was no mistaking the calm yet deliberate demeanor that made this incident no bigger deal than it had to be.

I have had the good fortune to work for some excellent managers in my professional life. The lessons I learned were not always easy but I am grateful to the men and women who saw enough promise in me to assign responsibility for the most valuable of all business resources – people. Regardless of the environment, business organizations large and small can realize tremendous success if they manage their people resources wisely. I have seen this proven over and over again in my career. And I'm not talking about coddling people or cajoling them to get their best work or loyalty. I'm talking about the application of solid management principles that bring out the best in workers because they feel valued and respected. I am glad to have had management experiences in a variety of industries and business environments. It gave me so many opportunities to learn or reaffirm basic skills and knowledge that could lead to business results, job satisfaction and even career advancement and longevity. Whether it has been formal management development classes taught at a huge worldwide corporation or discussing operational strategy over a beer with the CEO of a small consulting firm, all of these experiences have contributed to the base of knowledge and understanding I enjoy and put into practice each day I work.

Just as many other endeavors in life, the learning never ends. This book is simply a stop on the journey to reflect on a work life that has been both challenging and rewarding. It is also a way for me to say thank you to the many people, in both my professional and personal life, that have helped and supported me over the years. With a hunger to keep learning and surrounded by good people, I'm certain that anyone can become successful and achieve their goals but you have to be willing to adapt to change and keep your ego in check. The best managers I have encountered have a passion for their work and compassion for their people. They have a sense of urgency but never seem to panic. They focus on results and not just effort. Above all, they continually strive for a healthy balance between work and life responsibilities. "Everything in moderation," my father used to say. I've lost my way at times, but having a solid foundation to return to has been my salvation.

Whether this book provides new learning or simply helps you to confirm or fine-tune your own methods, I hope you will use it as just one more resource to add to your arsenal.

Throughout the book, I will provide some "words of wisdom" I have collected over the years. They serve as quick reminders of some concepts for success that have stuck with me and helped bring me back on track whenever veering off course. Look for the Celtic knot symbol to see them and there is also an appendix listing them all.

 BE SMART ENOUGH TO KNOW WHAT YOU *DON'T* KNOW.

Introduction

Whether you are presenting an employee with a bonus for producing extraordinary results or terminating someone for failure to meet job requirements, it can ALWAYS be done with respect. Respect is the fundamental foundation that can, and should be used to support all management activities. *Managing With Respect* is a boundless and timeless concept. In other words, no matter what the environment (resources, and skills scarce or plentiful, business booming or in the ditch), you can depend on this concept in managing all circumstances and resources to meet your objectives. You don't have to change your management philosophy or style; you don't have to appear to be transparent or lose credibility to affect changes necessary to build, maintain or revamp your business.

Managing With Respect is an objective approach that provides a consistent base from which to start, operate, measure, revise or transform everything in your business. The stability and applicability of such an approach allows for success at all levels and over time, can even help increase trust, overall performance and innovation within your business relationships.

Most importantly, *Managing With Respect* is not limited to just personnel management. The concept and principles in this model support the entire organization, all processes, and all extended relationships (clients, suppliers, partners, etc.) at a variety of levels. Even though it can be a delicate balancing act, respect for one "tier" of the organization cannot be sacrificed for respect at another. For example, layoffs, salary reductions and other actions to reduce expenses are often viewed as disrespectful to the hard working people affected. However, to ignore an organization's financial difficulties would be equally disrespectful only at a different level and from a different perspective within the business. Under such circumstances, there is rarely a solution that will not have a negative impact somewhere in the organization or on individuals, but if actions and rationale are communicated in a respectful way, you have at least treated all factions consistently and with integrity.

So, in many ways, the title of this book could be, *"Managing With Respect For . . ."* and you fill in the blank with the appropriate item (or combination of items) such as:

1. Customers
2. Employees
3. Shareholders
4. Government Regulations
5. Impact on Other Internal Organizations
6. Community / Social Impact
7. Yourself
8. Many, many others

Consider all of these, every time, on every decision? IMPOSSIBLE!

This writing is given from a line manager's perspective, but the human resources or personnel department must always be a major resource and supportive function in any activities discussed here.

Why treat people with respect? In today's business world, individual employees would do well to think of themselves as "Me, Incorporated" because there is no one that can provide guaranteed employment and each person must take responsibility for their own "marketability." That doesn't mean that employers are the "bad guys" and this way of thinking about the employment relationship need not be adversarial. You better always be prepared to take care of yourself by keeping your business skills current and marketable. But I submit to you that there is a dimension of employment that has deteriorated and should be revived by both individuals and companies in America and around the world if we desire to have a productive environment that is characterized by both harmony and prosperity.

The concepts of loyalty and commitment without tangible reward are unpalatable to many, but extremely important to re-establish the trust and confidence most people need in order to operate at peak performance. And what about the individual pride and integrity we all expect our business leaders to have? We all want to have a comfortable feeling that the company's policies include the same level of integrity that we strive for as individuals. That doesn't mean that you will never get laid off because you have been a loyal employee for 25 years. Layoff, downsizing, or whatever name you want to give it, is a matter of business necessity, and not necessarily a disrespectful process. But I'm talking about the benefits of ensuring your company truly believes in respect for employees as people and professionals, not just as their most expensive resource. A company that is cognizant of its workers' intangible results can leverage that from both a business and human relations perspective. To achieve this, a company must also train managers to recognize this type of contribution and use sound judgment in determining how to utilize it. In any case, the individual employee is worthy of basic respect regardless of the company, country, or business circumstances.

Best of all, this model and its components are really nothing more than a return to the basics, including common sense and common decency. The simplicity of these concepts makes them easy to comprehend yet, when truly employed in the workplace they are powerful by virtue of their ability to provide an openness and honesty that has diminished in many of today's organizations. Even in today's complex world, there is still value in identifying and applying a basic approach to respect in human interactions.

Building a comprehensive understanding of any topic or discipline requires on-going (even lifelong) study and the ability to seek out meaningful information. In my business life experience, the vast majority of documents, presentations, emails, and all other written documentation have usually been too long. Therefore, this book will make every attempt to provide completeness and thorough description using a minimal amount of words. I've also found that one of the best ways to teach people is to have examples and illustrations, so as many of these as I could think of are included as well.

While I believe this model may be applied to many circumstances and environments, the chapters focus heavily on activities related to "people resource" management for two reasons:

1. My personal perspective that there is no more important dimension of management than effective people management
2. It is an area where I have enjoyed much professional success and personal satisfaction so I believe I can provide credible and meaningful information to the reader

Conclusion

People are both the most valuable and most expensive resource in a business, so treating each individual with respect makes a great deal of sense if you are to hire and keep your best investment working in a genuine way to help you succeed. Motivation, skills, and level of involvement can all wane over years so managers must be aware of this phenomenon and not ignore it. You don't want to lose the solid employees who have a good base of knowledge for two reasons. From a business perspective, you are better off with their knowledge, experience and commitment. From a human relations perspective, you want to treat people with respect for the efforts they have given you over the years because it keeps them engaged and motivated and it's simply the right thing to do. Retaining talented and dedicated people in your business is extremely difficult today, but I submit to you that it is not only tangible rewards (salary, bonus, stock options, etc.) that people find attractive. When competing in the world (and I mean literally the entire world) for employees, you just may have an edge if you can demonstrate how your business *"Manages With Respect."*

Throughout this book I will describe how the *Managing With Respect* model supports the conclusion I've made above and how you can leverage my experiences to help you identify your own set of practices that lead to operational excellence in a wide variety of management disciplines. Whether you manage people, projects, business processes or any combination, my goal in this writing is to illustrate how the application of these principles can help you to become a better manager.

BETTER TO AIM AT PERFECTION AND MISS IT, THEN AIM AT SOMETHING LESS AND HIT IT RIGHT ON THE HEAD

Chapter 1: Describing the Model

Foundation and Key Principles for Success

Armed with a solid understanding and commitment to the concept of respect, you may begin to employ the key principles that will guarantee your success in any environment. The foundation and principles (or competencies) will never change but the content and application of them may have to, based on the situation you are dealing with.

Figure 1 (below) is a relatively simple model for success that I created many years ago but continue to test in every situation I'm involved in. Its genesis is my actual experience including many successes and failures in business environments within major corporations and small businesses alike. The perspectives provided stem from interactions with knowledge workers and management at many levels, as well as from the viewpoint of practitioner and consultant. I will begin with an overview of the *Managing With Respect* model and its components then provide illustrations of how to use the principles in real life situations.

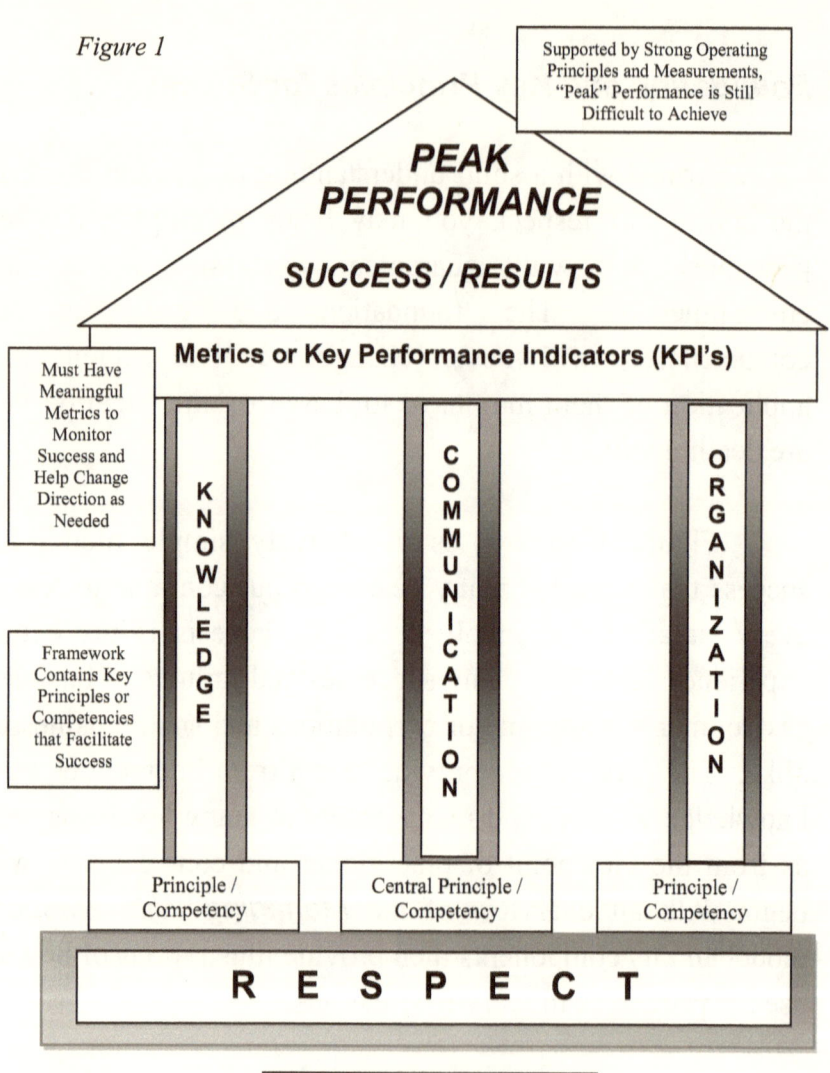

Figure 1

Supported by Strong Operating Principles and Measurements, "Peak" Performance is Still Difficult to Achieve

PEAK PERFORMANCE

SUCCESS / RESULTS

Metrics or Key Performance Indicators (KPI's)

Must Have Meaningful Metrics to Monitor Success and Help Change Direction as Needed

Framework Contains Key Principles or Competencies that Facilitate Success

K N O W L E D G E

C O M M U N I C A T I O N

O R G A N I Z A T I O N

Principle / Competency

Central Principle / Competency

Principle / Competency

R E S P E C T

Foundation Provides the Fundamental Basis for Everything You Do

Managing With Respect Model – Components Description

Respect is simply the mandatory foundation that allows the rest of the model to work for you. All relationships have the potential to include a set of "entities" and "tiers" of interaction that can make a simple situation more complex. Keep in mind that in these interactions, peers, the team or department, management, the organization, the company, clients, business partners and you (i.e., anyone who is a "stakeholder"), are all worthy of basic respect. That doesn't mean that all people affected during a complex decision will feel good, but treating everyone with respect during the process will certainly help when it comes time to accept the facts and move on.

Whereas respect for the law, company policies, department procedures and other "rules" are often black and white, respect for people is strewn with shades of gray. And as important as it is to respect the documented guidelines in any environment, it is the ability to demonstrate real respect for people that will earn us the most rewarding results. Make no mistake about it, there are ways to present an employee with a $10,000 bonus and show little respect. At the same time, it is also very feasible to terminate an employee and do it in such a way that the person doesn't lose respect in the process.

Throughout the course of this book, I will attempt to illustrate how respect provides the foundation that is so crucial for support of the entire model. However, as much as

17

I believe respect is a fundamental principle in all interactions, it is also true that respect can be lost as a result of actions and behaviors. While relationships with people and entities should begin with respect, that doesn't mean they will always end that way.

Knowledge is power. I know it's an old saying and to some it may seem cliché, but in this information age, it has never been more true. With more data and information available to us than ever before, the ability to actually find what you need, assess it for relevance and assimilate it in a timely fashion for practical use in your professional or personal life can be a daunting process. In fact, it is absolutely essential that we remember to read and research with the utmost discrimination or run the risk of basing decisions on faulty or incomplete information. Information "overload" is real and can cripple one's ability to acquire the knowledge they really need. *Knowing what you need to know* is more than half the battle today. Being smart enough to know what you DON'T know is also a valuable skill. "Informed" decisions are "effective" decisions.

My description of knowledge includes, but is certainly not limited to one's subject matter understanding of business process, technology, marketing, sales, industries, government, non-profit organizations, and thousands of other categories needed for success in your job and even at home. But, a solid knowledge (or understanding) of people is an equally, if not more important bank of "data" that is needed to facilitate success. There are many individuals who experience great success with their ability to acquire, process, retain and utilize data, turning it into usable information. Fewer people are able to take a myriad of information from a variety of time periods or sources and create something new with it (i.e., innovation). And even more rare are the people who are innovators of both process AND people. No one will be a master at all of this all the time, but there is nothing wrong with striving for it.

There is a fundamental principle that says you should always, "manage from strength." Well, there is nothing that makes you a stronger manager than having a great deal of knowledge.

One more note on acquiring and leveraging knowledge. The best database and processor you can have is your own brain, so keep it sharp and take time to consciously consider the accumulation and use of your "intellectual capital." This is a key resource that only you have ready access to, so leverage it when appropriate and find ways to ensure its reliability.

Organization skills are invaluable in today's complex and busy world. Whatever you seek to achieve, your ability to organize tasks, strategies, information, time (calendar), physical objects and even intangible things like emotions (anger, fear, frustration, etc.), can provide an effective way of life that creates satisfaction and self confidence. In discussing the "Knowledge" component above, I touched on how important it is to be able to summon the right information quickly. Organization makes that possible. For many years now, "time management" has been a hot topic for business people around the world. Companies have built entire consulting practices, products and services based on better time management, and organization is a major part of what must occur to realize more efficiency regarding your time. This principle is not referring to the way a business is organized but in fact, the reader just may find some correlation as you read on and begin to understand the efficiency that can come as a result of meaningful organization.

At times, you might find yourself getting caught up in "organizing for the sake of organization." The debate about whether a clean desk is the sign of a healthy mind or a sick one will rage on forever. Just remember to do what works best for you, be flexible enough to adapt your methods based on your environment and be open-minded enough to swap organization techniques that are better no matter how long you have been using them. The key is to always make sure your efforts to organize are yielding benefits. Quicker access to information should result in greater productivity; the ability to get more done in the same amount of time. The tools available today to help you not only organize, but even automate some of your work are well worth the time they take to learn. Trial and error as well as brainstorming with others will help you to find the right fit for you.

Communication is the central principle of the model because even though you can discuss it and illustrate it independently, it is the competency that allows you to culminate all others to achieve your goal. Described more vividly, if this model was an arch, communication would truly be the "keystone."

Make no mistake about it – communication is hard work! But some of the critical tasks you will perform to ensure success will involve planning how, when, what and why you communicate. Even the words used to compliment an employee for a job well done should be chosen wisely and delivered with sincerity, or not at all. In fact, those that may be somewhat unsure of their own communication skills, take note. The most important element of communication is not the words you choose or how eloquently they are delivered. It is the intent and genuine honesty with which they are dispensed that is most important.

Finally, even though I haven't highlighted it as a separate "component" of the model, another key element is the ability to define and implement meaningful measurements or *Metrics*. Also referred to as KPI's or *Key Performance Indicators*, pretty much everything you do and/or change needs to be measured or evaluated so you can identify strengths, areas needing improvement and whether or not certain programs or projects are affordable in your environment and are producing an acceptable ROI (Return On Investment).

Now that you have a better understanding of the model's components, let's discuss how to put those principles and competencies into practice. The following chapters will provide guidance and illustrations of how to utilize the model in a variety of everyday management activities.

Illustrative Example

As much as possible, I will inject my personal experiences into this work to illustrate how the model and principles work in "the real world." You may not always agree with my assessment, but there is no better teacher than experience, so I offer these cases in the hope that many readers will relate to them.

Call center management (also known as Customer Service Center and Help Desk) is a challenging environment indeed. But there is no better environment to show how using the *Managing With Respect* model can help provide a solid base from which to build effectiveness and high performance.

For five years, I managed people and projects needed to bring an internal 24x7 corporate "help desk" organization from a problem report and dispatch function to a problem "resolving" function that was a much more valuable resource to internal IT systems users and second level support teams. We had to start by building the base of *knowledge*. Agents that staffed the desk were capable, but had never been required or held accountable for resolving even the simplest problems. Using computer based training modules, formal classes and our own technical and application support teams; we scheduled mandatory learning activities to raise the level of expertise.

The *organization* skills needed to pull the training schedule together might illustrate this *Managing With*

Respect principle well enough, but even more important to us was organizing the results. You see, not only were we raising the level of expertise to raise the bar on support services provided, but we also had to become a more efficient organization (i.e., provide more and better service with fewer resources). The unfortunate reality was that we had to reduce our department headcount. Defining the criteria to be used for determining who would stay and who would go had to be done with a great deal of thought and consideration for both performance in the "classroom" and other skills and abilities that could contribute to our success.

You might think that all of this activity, conducted in a relatively short period of time, would create a very negative environment with low morale. I'd be lying if I said there weren't some bad feelings, but our planning and execution was supported by a solid foundation of *respect* and this absolutely helped everyone through the process. We began by clearly communicating as much as we possibly could about the mandatory education, expectations for attendance and completion and the fact that some would not "make the cut." From a *metrics* perspective, we had all the data we needed from tests conducted within the training sessions. In addition, we implemented monthly one-on-one job performance evaluations to provide both objective and subjective feedback to each and every employee. This frequent and brief yet thorough *communication* provided employees and management a common document and forum for discussion that illustrated fairness within a difficult process.

The results were quite good for both business and people and this experience allowed me to test the soundness of the model and principles. I'll talk more about this environment in the upcoming chapters as there is much more to be learned.

What Would You Do?

Before you dive into learning how to apply the *Managing With Respect* model, I'm going to provide a real world situation for you to keep in mind as you read the next 14 chapters. I'm sure you will have some initial reaction and opinions on how to handle this set of circumstances, but please don't skip to the end of the book and read how I handled it. Use your interpretation and understanding of the following principles to develop your own strategy. Obviously, there is no right or wrong answer but if your understanding of the *Managing With Respect* model allows you to realize different methods for resolving issues that are more effective, you will have broadened your base of knowledge and increased versatility for managing tough problems. Here's the situation:

One year ago, you were the relatively new manager of a department and one of your employees had an ongoing issue that preceded you. When receiving turnover from the former leader you learned that this employee, a 20 year veteran of the company, felt he had been treated unfairly regarding his desire to move to a different job within the organization. His performance ratings had been satisfactory and although his career development plan stated that he aspired to this other position, he clearly lacked many of the

24

skills needed to be successful and had not responded adequately to counseling regarding his current job. As a result, his management did not make him available to interview for the other job.

You began by having several discussions with the employee and eventually let him know you had reviewed the situation and were in agreement with his former manager's assessment. The employee decided to escalate several management levels until the site executive granted him the position he desired with the understanding that he had one year to prove his ability to be successful. Now, a year later, this employee is returning to his former assignment as directed by the executive. He has received an overall performance evaluation for the year that indicates marginal results but is considered satisfactory. The employee disagrees that he should be returned to his prior position but understands that the executive has the authority to make this call. He also contends that while not outstanding, his job performance indicates that he was successful in the new area. As he returns to your group you are concerned about the implications of this action on the individual, other members of the department and the even the larger organization.

As you read the following chapters, use your own knowledge base along with what you learn to compile a plan of action for the circumstances above. We'll revisit this situation and the actions I took at the end of the *"Pulling it All Together"* chapter.

DON'T FORGET *LONG-TERM PLANNING* WHEN FOCUSED ON SHORT-TERM RESULTS

Applying the Managing With Respect Model in the Real World

Chapter 2: Recruiting and Hiring

Recruiting and hiring the right talent in the 21st century is very different than 30 years ago, but equally, if not more crucial for an organization's success. Today's managers must be aware that the candidate pool is more diverse and global in nature than ever before. This represents both a challenge and an extraordinary opportunity for the manager looking to hire people who can really make a difference in their company. Having a solid process for recruiting and hiring will serve your business in both the *short term* with higher individual *performance* and the *long term* as you *retain* that talented person. Let's explore how the *Managing With Respect* model and its components apply to the activity of *Recruiting and Hiring*.

RESPECT

With regard to recruiting and hiring people, do we really need to expand on how and why candidates should be respected? Unfortunately, yes we do. How many company representatives attend job fairs and recruiting events with an attitude of superiority? Sure, you hold the power to hire or not, but you are also often the first impression that potential employees get of a company. You should always be cognizant of this and demonstrate by your actions that you have an unconditional respect for your own company as well as for the people who are interested enough to learn more about it.

Respect for your company includes understanding and embracing its beliefs and values, and representing them in your words and actions, especially when dealing with people outside your firm. Even the remotest possibility that your lack of understanding or commitment to these values will show through, and thereby diminish the effectiveness of your campaign with job seekers.

KNOWLEDGE

Let's assume you are armed with a comprehensive list of your company's attributes, including tangible and intangible benefits of becoming an employee. How does one prepare for the opportunity to meet one or more prospective employees? Some feel that preparation beyond their own work experience is not necessary. Seasoned HR (human resources) or other company recruiters may feel that their knowledge of the company and the fact that they hold the hiring tickets give them all the knowledge they need. But knowing the candidates (individually by curriculum vitae or resume) or the environment (college or university academic programs, etc.) illustrates that you recognize the unique nature of each person or group. Even a high level understanding of the people or groups that you will encounter can be turned into good conversation and mutual respect that may be the difference in the level of interest generated for your company.

You also need to ensure a thorough knowledge of your company's hiring practices, including "Do's and "Don'ts" associated with all the steps in the process. If you are the hiring manager, you don't have to become the HR expert, but you should be able to answer simple questions about the hiring process and have a resource readily available to find answers to more complex questions. Most companies will document such information in a "handbook" so you don't have to memorize the material, but you should at least know where to find it.

ORGANIZATION

Organizing time and materials needed to ensure success in recruiting events cannot be underestimated. Showing up late, looking like you slept in your suit and not knowing where you are supposed to be does not bode well for your credibility or the reputation of your company. I once attended a recruiting event where we were given the authority to extend job offers that day if we deemed the person to be an exceptional hire. This was excellent empowerment for the management team but without organizing our approach and the process we would follow under these circumstances, the chances of our looking dull when making such an offer was actually very high unless we did our homework.

Prior to the event we determined that if one of us thought we had an outstanding person, we would immediately ask another manager to do a second interview. We also had to be prepared with details of work location, salary, benefits and any other questions that might come up. Some of this information was standard, but we actually built a simple spreadsheet that allowed us to insert variable information for a particular candidate and produce a basic document showing the person details of salary and benefits, including signing bonus, stock options, 401K potential savings, etc. This could be created in a few minutes on a laptop and shared with the candidate. It even allowed us to perform 'what if' scenarios should we get into negotiation or a competitive situation that day. This is just an example, but the point is that organizing your work activities can indeed provide a real advantage for you and your company.

COMMUNICATION

So, you've built your base of knowledge of candidates and the environment you're entering for a successful recruiting experience. You have anticipated all needs using outstanding organization techniques. Congratulations! You will fail miserably unless you can also do an effective job of communication! Good planning and due diligence are absolutely key ingredients for success but the ability to engage in succinct and meaningful dialogue, whether it is with a group or one-on-one, gives you a distinct competitive advantage. If you are already accomplished at such communication, your job is easier. However, if you have struggled in the past with effective communications in a similar environment, you must prepare yourself or run the risk of losing credibility regardless of other strengths you and your organization have to offer.

Verbal communication effectiveness is not only what you say, but how you say it. And, don't forget that "listening" is an important communication skill that, if practiced, can serve you well in many encounters. We all know people who seem to communicate more effectively than others. It comes naturally to some and others must really work at it. Bottom line; more often than not, communication involves hard work and conscious effort. Those who leave critical communication to chance are risking more than they realize.

Finally, here is one more note about communication as it relates to recruiting and hiring. What and how you communicate during these key processes will often be a difference maker in a person's mind so you owe it to them and yourself to be as honest as possible. The goal is to hire the brightest and the best, but you cannot lose sight of the subsequent objective of "keeping" those good people. Granted, when you are recruiting, you can't predict what will happen after the new employee starts, but if you set realistic expectations; the likelihood of their being disappointed will be diminished greatly. Now that you and the new employee are at the height of excitement, don't let momentum slide. It's time to focus on Orientation.

 COMMUNICATION IS *HARD WORK*

Chapter 3: Appropriate Orientation

Often times, the hours of challenging work associated with recruiting and hiring leaves people mentally exhausted so this is NOT the time to start pulling together a comprehensive employee orientation plan. When new people are left to learn for themselves, it can lead to frustration and the thought that the company is disorganized and doesn't care.   There is no simple process can't be established, documented and agreed to by an organization well before employees show up for their first day of work. The benefits are two-fold. Firstly, you keep the momentum going for that enthusiastic new recruit, confirming for them that you called a well run, organized and therefore competitive organization really is.   Secondly, defining, executing and monitoring an orientation process gives you a much better chance that all new employees will get the benefit of the same information and resources. Here's how to do it.

RESPECT

Now that the hiring decision has been made, smart managers will continue to illustrate that the company knows how to treat people with respect which includes also setting the stage for expectations. Most managers want their new employees to get to work and start producing results as soon as possible and there is nothing wrong with that. But making sure the new person is armed with the necessary tools and information will also illustrate that you care about getting the job done correctly, not just keeping people busy.   Even experienced professionals who can "hit the ground running," may benefit from a mentor or work-buddy when they come into a new environment. All of this takes time and effort; two very valuable commodities in your work life. But you have to keep believing that the investment will pay off with both tangible and intangible results. In fact, you owe it to the employee, yourself and the organization to conduct effective and timely orientation because it is also a good way to spot when you've made a bad hire. There are obviously many scenarios possible here, but the ultimate result is that it is better to identify a problem early and address it than ignore it and hope it goes away. It takes courage to review and address such issues with brand new people but avoiding it not respectful to anyone involved.

KNOWLEDGE

Any good employee orientation program must include facts, usually at a summary level, about your company's human resources programs and benefits. In fact, many organizations require that employees attend both an HR orientation session and a line-management conducted business orientation. However you choose to present this information to your newest team members, make sure you have the most current and accurate facts available. Offering your "best guess" about the details of complex HR programs may be a noble gesture but confusion and inconsistency in delivering this information is bound to occur, doing no one any good, and possibly leading to lost credibility.

From a business perspective, once again the key is to impart as many meaningful facts as possible to ensure a solid foundation from which the employee may begin to build their specific knowledge bank quickly. Use "subject matter experts" (SME's) to provide information, making sure the content and level of detail is appropriate. Assigning "work buddies" and/or mentors can work well, but be sure to have a well thought out plan already in place to meet the needs of the "trainee."

Always work with facts and defer to the experts if there is any doubt. On the other hand, simply handing new employees a list of internal web sites with no explanation or guidance may be equally risky. Find a delivery method that blends facts with helpful guidance for quick and accurate use, and you will be doing both the new employee and the business a favor.

ORGANIZATION

As stated above, having the facts is critically important, but taking the time to ensure a well thought out and deliberate process to deliver the facts is just as crucial for success. I created such a program for a large information technology organization where our hiring included entry-level professionals, senior technical staff and everything in-between. With this kind of diversity, from an experience level or what I call a "business maturity" perspective, the program had to meet the needs of savvy professionals as well as anxious young college graduates. I built simple "control books" (one of my favorite organization techniques), complete with a documented process, timeline, checklists and other helpful information resources.

The process was a compilation of ideas and suggestions from all managers who would be asked to use it, so when presenting the books and process to them, the likelihood of whole-hearted adoption was significantly increased. Of course I knew there would be some managers who would have additional orientation tasks and information for their new employees, but as long as they executed the "core process" completely (all required tasks) and in a timely fashion, they would be fine when it came to collecting monthly achievement against our 100% target. And by the way, no matter how elementary the metrics, monitoring and feedback will ensure you have consistent execution and will quickly identify any deviations so you may take corrective action and get back on track.

COMMUNICATION

Arguably, this component is the most crucial in the employee orientation process. Success may be achieved by applying the principles above and then using a blend of formal and informal communication techniques for an overall well-rounded implementation. Never take lightly the impact that these early communications can have on new employees. Whether they are experienced professionals or right out of college, the message you convey and how you convey it can stay with people for a long time. You owe it to yourself, the employee and the company to provide meaningful information in the shortest period of time to facilitate maximum productivity and show, from the very first meeting, that no one benefits if the orientation process drags on attempting to teach newcomers everything they'll need to know for the next year. Provide the high level info, make sure they know where to get help, and then put them to work!

In my second management assignment, I took over a department of people whom I had worked with, in varying degrees, before. As I conducted one-on-one meetings to get to know each of the people, one in particular refused to meet with me. No reason was given by the employee and despite my efforts; I could not get underneath what was causing this behavior. Finally, I suggested we meet on "neutral ground" instead of my office, and so we sat down in a conference room and, at long last, had an open discussion.

As it turns out, several years earlier I had encountered this employee when presenting material in a class for our organization. I remembered the class but had no idea that my communication that day led this person to believe I was looking down on the people in the class and had a feeling of superiority. In my mind, nothing could be further from the truth, but obviously I had done something that left this kind of impression with this person. Whatever the failure in that initial communication between me and this person, it left a lasting impression that definitely affected both productivity and trust in the relationship until we could discuss openly and resolve. I'm happy to say we did resolve this and went on to a successful manager / employee relationship thereafter. But I did learn a valuable lesson to be extremely aware of not only what you communicate, but how, especially when dealing with people you may not know that well.

You can never be sure what people are thinking or what their expectations are, so you need to hone your communication skills over time, learning from mistakes and seeking out input regularly from everyone you feel will provide honest feedback.

 DEVELOP *BUSINESS MATURITY*

Chapter 4: Setting Expectations

A successful business project almost always starts with a solid plan. A thoughtful approach to "planning" job performance standards and expectations follows the same logic. Most managers have a documented set of responsibilities for each job; some more detailed than others. But unless you also define (and quantify where possible) the expected results for employees, you will miss the opportunity to actually get the results you truly want as well as the ability to motivate and praise people for outperforming their objectives. If you want individuals to produce business results that align with the organization's overall objectives, you must define how those pieces fit together as well as how employees will meet, fail to meet, or exceed their individual goals. This is not a trivial process and unfortunately in today's world, where business needs can change frequently, maintaining a current and meaningful version of job responsibilities and performance criteria can drive a lot of workload for managers. Your biggest challenge will be to understand where there are "gaps" in performance and then quantify the benefits that may be obtained by investing the time and effort needed to define expected output. Here's how the foundation and principles apply.

RESPECT

If you have ever been taken by surprise at feedback presented in your formal performance review, chances are that expectations had something to do with the divergence. I would much rather miss a goal because the expectation was too high, than miss it because I didn't understand what it was.

It just makes good sense to define expectations and check periodically to make sure everyone understands. You get more predictable results from both a business and people perspective when you set clear expectations and manage to them consistently. Some people say that their best boss has been the one with the highest expectations because she or he challenged them and provided real opportunity for better performance. I would have to agree as in my experiences, the jobs with the biggest challenges were also the ones where I worked the hardest and got the most recognition. Setting expectations and communicating clearly and consistently is absolutely setting a solid foundation for results.

KNOWLEDGE

Obviously, if you are responsible for defining employee job responsibilities and performance expectations, you better have a good understanding of what the job entails. This knowledge may be obtained by actually doing the job or through close examination and analysis of what skills and abilities are needed to execute the job with proficiency.

Let's take a moment to recognize two distinct trains of thought on "knowing" how to do a job and supervising people that do it. Many people believe that if you haven't actually performed a job in an area you are managing, you cannot be successful. "Walking a mile in one's moccasins" is valuable indeed, but not an absolute necessity to produce results for both business and people. The key to achieving success when managing an area you never worked in before is, "being smart enough to know what you *don't* know."

With this in mind you may begin to learn what you need to ensure you and your employees are collaborating at the correct level to execute efficiently and with desired results. If you simply ignore what you don't know and let the people do what they have always done, you may or may not be successful, but you will certainly *NOT* be in control, and you may actually lose credibility and the respect of your people in your role as manager, coach and mentor. Remember, most people will have a basic respect for your authority from day one, but that status will certainly diminish over time if you are viewed as someone who is not willing to learn, if for no other reason than to be able to empathize with employees' day-to-day struggles and triumphs.

So, don't be ashamed or hide your lack of experience. Rather, make sure people know where you can contribute the most and where you need (and want) to learn more so you can maximize your effectiveness as the leader of the team. Be sincere and committed to learning from your subordinates but don't lose sight of the fact that you are also the supervisor and ultimately you're responsible to appraise their job performance. Building a strong base of knowledge and continuous learning allows you to provide meaningful feedback and illustrates your respect for the people in your charge.

ORGANIZATION

Even the most knowledgeable and experienced supervisor needs to establish an organized approach to ensure consistency for the team. For example, many seasoned managers can tell you, without hesitation, the difference between extraordinary performance in a senior-level vs. entry-level position. But unless those differences are documented and available to the people, they may never get reviewed or discussed. Not to mention that over time, expectations may change based on business needs and if you haven't created that "baseline," you will undoubtedly have created an environment of assumption and confusion.

On several occasions, I created performance criteria documents that detailed requirements for each job responsibility, every level of job and every possible performance level. In some cases, this took a tremendous amount of time but the benefits were numerous. First and foremost was the ability to sit down one-on-one with employees and use the document to facilitate understanding for current job performance, career opportunity and a host of other purposes. Next, is the advantage of sharing this information with peer managers to improve consistency when communicating expectations to employees across the organization. In some cases, defining performance criteria for soft skills such as verbal communication, teamwork, etc., were extracted and used in completely different areas of the company.

Side Note: As a regular employee, remember that most companies own anything you create. In the example of my performance criteria documentation, all of it was considered "intellectual property" owned by my employer at the time. You can certainly claim that any such work represents your personal accomplishment, but you most likely will not own the material or have any right to use outside the confines of your enterprise.

Here's one every manager who writes annual evaluations will appreciate. If done properly, the documented performance criteria become an excellent reference to help you document results. I don't advocate a complete "cut and paste" approach but as long as you have already spent a great deal of time and effort documenting performance expectations, it is perfectly appropriate to then go back and use that information in describing the actual performance of an employee. More about assessing performance in another chapter but suffice it to say, don't document expectations and then never use it again!

Finally, in the call center environment I mentioned earlier, we were deep into a transformation from a dispatch function to a true first level "help desk" when I created the performance criteria document. An unintended but effective use of this work was in justification of the department budget for the following year. Annual review and justification of headcount, training dollars, equipment, etc., was an extremely detailed process but the definition of what benefits and value could be expected from our department was bolstered by this comprehensive document.

COMMUNICATION

Knowing the individual job responsibilities, linking them to organizational goals and documenting consistent and comprehensive performance criteria will help bring you much closer to actually getting the results you need to be successful. So don't stop short of the most important step, effective communication of expectations. Even with a solid document, what you communicate and how, is critically important to ensuring an understanding. When you have understanding, it is more likely you will see motivation, if not enthusiasm, on the part of employees to shine.

Most people will appreciate having these performance guidelines. It is important to discuss that there is subjectivity and judgment involved in the evaluation process and it is not equivalent to calculating a grade in a class by averaging up all test scores during the semester and using the result to determine your overall standing. The exception may be jobs where performance is completely objective and quantifiable (e.g., producing 'x' number of items per hour, etc.). But even those jobs will have areas of importance that require subjective criteria be applied, so don't shy away from discussing with employees how that performance will be assessed.

Using examples of performance along with the documented criteria, as well as indicating where there may be variables applied to help distinguish results of many people, will help employees understand expectations and how to excel. Some organizations use peer feedback or other "organization-wide" performance indicators as part of their appraisal process. Be sure to factor these into the communication with employees so they may see how it will be considered in their annual review.

I once took over leadership of a department where there was a monthly "quality" metric with a goal of 90% that had never been achieved. Just before taking the reins, my manager informed me that he was raising the objective to 95%. This took me a little by surprise but even though the team had not been able to achieve the lower target, this new level made good business sense, so I went off to figure out how to get it done. To make a long story short, the team achieved the new target within 6 months and sustained it for years thereafter, often exceeding the 95% goal for months at a time. In this case, the critical success factor was related to setting expectations, but it was the defining of "ownership" that made it all work.

Each employee was assigned a clear set of responsibilities and a business area that they would "own." The 95% quality objective was the same for everyone but each person was now able to focus their efforts on managing all aspects of quality for a subset of the department's work. These were experienced people so the basics were not a problem, but where it became tricky was in managing dependencies (i.e., the work product of other organizations that was needed for our processes), which they were not used to doing. Now, they had to find ways to ensure the quality of their own work as well as the work of others. Needless to say, when you have a 95% target documented in your performance plan and you know you can't achieve it alone, it's a little nerve racking. The good news was, at least you only had to worry about your section of the business and not the whole department; that was the boss' problem. More on this experience in the following section on "Providing Feedback."

 IDENTIFY, MANAGE AND CLOSE THE *GAPS*

Chapter 5: Providing Feedback

This chapter goes hand-in-hand with the preceding chapter on "Setting Expectations" so I'll be continuing many of the thought processes started there. If you haven't read the previous chapter, please take a few minutes to do this before you move on as this will increase the meaningfulness of this section.

When it comes to providing feedback, I have found that brief is best, frequent is better than rarely and honesty is absolutely essential. Informal is just as powerful as formal feedback, but always document after informal to ensure you can track progress and/or prove by example to superiors, actions you wish to take. As stated above, doing a good job of setting expectations will greatly enhance the feedback process and hopefully, minimize surprises - and that's absolutely one of the goals here. No one likes surprises, especially at performance review time, but there will always be different perspectives so understanding that this process is less than perfect is a good place to start. As a manager, *what* you communicate is obviously important, but *how* you communicate it is even more crucial to ensuring the understanding (not necessarily agreement) that you seek. Let's take a look at how the foundation and three principles apply.

RESPECT
As powerful as providing feedback can be, if it is delivered the wrong way, you may do more harm than good. It almost sounds like something you would see in a movie or

a TV sitcom, but employees have actually been demoted, disciplined and even fired by email. I'm not sure there is any good rationale for doing business this way but even if you have a very emotionally charged situation, I suggest you do your best to treat people with dignity no matter what the circumstances. In the grand scheme of things, it is your credibility and reputation that will suffer even if you find a way to rationalize the action.

KNOWLEDGE

Once again, if you are responsible for providing feedback, and want it to be meaningful, you should strive for unquestionable credibility with regard to job responsibilities and how actual performance is being assessed. For example, it's great to have objective data for certain job responsibilities but it is not wise to utilize such information from reporting systems if you really don't have some understanding as to how the data was gathered and analyzed. Make sure you are well versed in how all performance feedback mechanisms or processes are executed and be able to confidently discuss the reliability of any tool or application used. Make sure you have read and interpreted data correctly and do a "reasonability check" wherever possible to avoid an embarrassing moment or worse with employees. Don't assume that just because you are the manager, and maybe have even done the job before, that you still know every aspect better than the employee now performing it. Even if you are positive you could perform every job just as well or better than your employees, your challenge now is to find ways to get it accomplished through the people.

Newer employees will undoubtedly have less insight and benefit from more specific direction on how to do things. Seasoned staff members may benefit more from a discussion at a higher level of execution or empowerment. For example, let's say you have two employees who are both failing to deliver their weekly activity reports on time each Friday. One employee is last year's college hire and one is a five year veteran. You might instruct the new employee to start keeping a daily journal with a few notes at the end of the work day and take no longer than 5 minutes to complete it. Then, on Friday at 4:45 pm, review and edit those notes and copy and paste them into a complete weekly report. There is no room for creativity here, but you know this will work and you know that the newbie needs a specific method to be successful. By the way, if you assign a specific procedure like this and never follow up to make sure it's being done, get ready to be disappointed.

You may or may not know why there is now an issue with the more senior employee's timely completion of this report, but you must address it. This person might be turned off by such a specific solution as they have been around long enough to know about managing time and doing weekly reports. But they might not understand how their report is actually used after they send it to you. In this situation, you might explain to the person that you review their report along with others and often use them in preparing your monthly status presentation to upper management. You could explain how this information lends credibility to the monthly rollup because it allows middle management to see the real department performance and problems from the "front lines."

Discussing this process with the employee illustrates that you know they have a slightly higher level of "business maturity." Knowing your people will allow you to address problems in the most meaningful and effective way.

Your feedback obviously depends on understanding the circumstances surrounding the issue, but whatever you provide as feedback had better be sincere and honest. If there is no other reason for the weekly report than, "the boss wants it done that way," tell the people that's the way it is. Don't try and snow them; they will know.

ORGANIZATION

Do yourself, your management and your employees a favor by organizing your thoughts BEFORE delivering feedback. Informal and brief feedback sessions are very effective but if they are "off the cuff, shooting from the hip," or come from any other cliché area of your person or wardrobe, stop and think about the effect they will have. If you see an opportunity to pat a person on the back, you want to take it, and quickly for maximum benefit. But if taking a few minutes to validate or even add substance to the accolade is possible, you may just end up with feedback that is even more meaningful and powerful.

For example, you see that someone has worked hard all day long without taking a break and you tell an employee, "Nice job today." But what if you took a few extra minutes to quantify the "nice job" and deliver the feedback as, "Nice job on clearing the backlog we accumulated this week. Your hard work helped us to catch up despite higher volumes."

49

This is not only more powerful because the employee knows that "you know" what the heck is going on, but your recognition is also reinforcing specific expectations already spelled out in their job description.

Formal reviews, especially those that are used as criteria for salary increase and promotion opportunities, should always be preceded by a great deal of planning and thought before being prepared and delivered. Today's jobs are often performed by knowledge-workers with responsibilities that include a great deal of subjectivity when it comes to assessing performance. Defining objective performance criteria in jobs will help form a foundation for discussion and even a starting point for more subjective assessment. Regardless of how you define job responsibilities and the criteria for meeting them, *always, always, always* have your facts together before providing feedback. Validate objective data to ensure it is accurate and consistent. Review and double-check your subjective conclusions to make sure they make sense.

Unfortunately, job performance feedback is often done quickly and incompletely. Some managers consider the process a "necessary evil" that takes them away from their "real" work. Others simply don't have time to do as thorough a job as they would like. Human resources departments stand guard and slap management on the wrist when they are late with required annual reviews and management continues to try and find ways to make the process meaningful yet easier and faster to execute. There is no easy solution to this dilemma, but in addition to organizing yourself for greater efficiency and effectiveness, the key to success lies in your ability to communicate.

COMMUNICATION

We have actually touched on some communication methods above but when it comes to providing feedback, there is no more important job than thinking through what to communicate and how to present it to ensure understanding. As a new manager I once prepared a performance review for an employee that I considered to be marginal regarding his job responsibilities. We sat in my office for over two hours discussing and disagreeing on the details of the assessment. The fact is I was never going to get the employee to agree with my appraisal. What I needed to ensure was his understanding, both of the criteria used and the expectations going forward. Agreement is always nice, but not the main objective when providing feedback.

Too often, people don't stop to create a deliberate plan for communication. However, when it is apparent that you have taken a thoughtful approach, people will often recognize it as a sign of respect and professionalism. In one of my assignments I had many employees that came from another company and were not used to a structured process for job performance feedback. They were skeptical when I explained our process at the start, but they were pleasantly surprised when we actually delivered what we said we would later that year. They respected the fact that the company would allow managers to take time to compile such detailed and thorough reports of job performance for each individual. Regardless of what the overall appraisal stated, the initial point

51

communicated to each person was that we care enough to do a thorough job and the time spent is indicative of our commitment to our people.

Remember the team that had to manage their own work as well as influencing the work of others to achieve the quality objective? We made it because we executed solid business, technical and communication skills consistently over time. And if you were thinking that the team was initially apprehensive about having to manage the work of others, you would be right! In fact, this change in direction had some people flat out angry. Now that it was communicated *what* we were going to do to achieve 95%, I had to communicate *how* to accomplish it. Over time, I met with groups and individuals to discuss issues and how to resolve or simply influence movement in the right direction. I encouraged people to meet frequently, often face-to-face, with their peers to explain the objectives and seek out collaboration. At the same time, I was meeting with my peer managers to do the same and I made sure my team knew it was going on.

Finally, when it came to performance review time, that 95% figure looming large, I was able to communicate to the individual employees their overall objective attainment along with my subjective assessment of their efforts. Together, these factors were used to determine their performance against that goal. They came to understand that the 95% objective was not a hammer to be wielded until we achieved it. As long as we were making concerted efforts, progress was being made and we could recognize those efforts in a variety of ways. In other words, the performance criteria used to assess "quality" was multi-dimensional. Despite the fact that there was a hard and fast objective figure as the target, the subjective nature of the work needed to get there was factored in. Over time, and with many team and individual communication sessions, people began to understand how to manage this challenging responsibility. These efforts were rewarded in both team celebrations and individual recognition. That brings us to the next area we'll examine – Recognition and Rewards.

 CONDUCT REGULAR FOLLOW-UP; *INSPECT WHAT YOU EXPECT*

Chapter 6: *Employee Development and Career Planning*

As a new manager, I remember feeling quite inadequate in the area of employee development and career planning. After all, I was relatively young and new to the corporate business world myself, so how was I to help create professional development plans for all my people when my own career experiences were so few? Over time I learned that it must start with a genuine desire to help, a commitment to listening and the ability to assist people identify realistic goals, objectives and timeframes. Remember too, that documenting career goals and planning development activities can and should be very much a tailored process, based on the individual's needs and aspirations with consideration for the business or company requirements. Done properly, skills development and career planning can help both the individual employee and the organization profit. If employee and manager understand the importance of this relationship going into a career planning process, the execution of that plan should yield mutually beneficial results, and it doesn't get any better than that! Now, let's apply the model to this process.

RESPECT

Unlike job performance plan preparation, career planning can be a much more personal process and requires significant involvement on the part of the employee if it is to be meaningful. In a large company, the HR department may monitor compliance to having development activities or career plans documented for all employees. It is a legitimate measurement because a business makes a significant investment in people and it only makes sense to keep those resources both skilled and motivated. But this can often drive managers to meet the requirement levied by HR at the expense of a quality plan that really serves the individual's needs and desires. By making sure the employee is fully engaged in this process, you stand a much better chance of producing a plan for development that actually gets executed.

I used to always make sure 100% of my team members had current development plans, and I thought they had some pretty realistic goals and activities. But over the years, it was apparent that many of the plans never got completed. We had *planned the work* but not *worked the plan*. Over time, I got better at helping people to define realistic activities that they could maintain enthusiastic about. This helped somewhat but I also made sure employees knew was this. If the plan we develop doesn't get executed, I might be disappointed and the company may have squandered some resource, but the one who loses the most is you. For example, if your plan calls for enhancing technical skills by taking an online course paid for by the company, but you never complete it, that's a waste of money for the business but more significantly, a missed opportunity for you. Explaining the reality of development planning and getting the employee's sincere involvement and commitment to the process illustrates a healthy respect for the individual and the organization, and leads to more success.

KNOWLEDGE

The more you know about your employees' strengths and weaknesses, the better you are prepared to assist them in defining a meaningful and realistic set of plans for developing skills and attributes that will serve them well and align with their goals.

In one assignment, I had a department of employees that ranged in experience from new hire to 25 years. I was really struggling to help one of the veteran workers to define his career goals and objectives when I found an instrument that could be used for individuals to assess their own strengths, weaknesses and career objectives. I shared with the person that completing this tool might help identify something we missed or never thought of. He was polite enough in accepting the strategy but never completed the survey.

After 25 years in the company, this person wasn't interested in finding new ways to help him march up the ladder to higher level jobs. He simply wanted to keep his skills current to allow for continued success in his assignment and also seek out possible transfers to his home state, where he planned to retire in five years. My suggestion for completing the job skills and career interest inventory was sincere, but it was never going to be helpful for this particular employee. When I finally "heard" his real aspirations, we scheduled some appropriate technical and personal communication classes. We also documented the fact that he desired a transfer, if possible, and I made some inquiries regarding potential job opportunities in the location he desired. It was after I left that department that I heard the employee found a job in the location he wanted. The realistic plan helped him continue to contribute on his current job, and the documented career aspirations kept the desire to transfer locations out in the open, so when an opportunity did present itself, his management could be supportive and not surprised.

Truly knowing employees gets you in a great position to help develop skills and abilities that serve both the individual and the organization. But knowing the resources available and navigating your way through the internal processes required to execute a meaningful plan often takes a concerted effort. Like many other tasks, the more you do it, the better you get, so don't shy away from the hard work and obstacles you are bound to encounter. Overcoming difficulties allows you to meet the immediate goal of building a good plan, but it also increases your own base of personal experience and knowledge to be applied in the future.

For example, if a development activity for a team member involves working through the company's process for tuition reimbursement for the first time, you should definitely take steps to capture the procedures and any nuances that helped you accomplish this task. This future reference will allow you to be more efficient the next time. The knowledge you gain can also help you to make better decisions when contemplating which activities are best for a particular employee.

ORGANIZATION

Organizing information (like the tuition reimbursement program example above) is an invaluable habit to practice, especially as it relates to "non-core" department or team processes. What I mean here is that you may always have the latest sales figures, project status or department productivity data on the tip of your tongue because that information represents the majority of what's important to the business (i.e., your "core" work). But even if you have learned a great deal from work in other areas of your management responsibility, those details may fade away quickly because they are less of a priority as time goes on. However, when you need that information a year later and know that you had it at one time, there is nothing like the frustration of not being able to put your hands on it quickly. As I have said earlier, people with photographic memories may not have to worry about this scenario, but for us mere mortals, we need an organized approach to storing and accessing information.

In this age of information there are almost unlimited resources and tools to help you acquire, organize and utilize data for a variety of tasks. It takes a discriminating approach to ensure you gather the most relevant information and use the tool that is most appropriate for the job. I have been using spreadsheets since I first became a manager in 1981. I had no personal computer or software, but with a legal size sheet of paper and a pencil and ruler, I could easily map out a logical depiction of my team's information, including deadlines for performance reviews, development plan dates, salary planning, etc. for an entire year. Today's spreadsheet programs are incredibly powerful and easier to use than ever. Designed properly, just about any information you want to maintain, sort and summarize can be stored in a spreadsheet. If you are really adventurous and have the time and aptitude, today's database apps, such as Microsoft Access, can be used to improve on information storage, analysis and reporting capabilities. It will take some time to design your strategy, but when done, you are looking at a whole new level of flexibility and time-saving processes.

Actually, back in those early days of personal computing, I thought it would be great to automate my "personnel management" spreadsheet. The popular Lotus 123 spreadsheet tool seemed like a good way to accomplish this but I had no expertise in this area. So, just like when I was a kid, I decided to impose on my older brother for help. He was always a math whiz and now a programmer with more technical skills than I would ever have. He wrote a simple macro (mini-program) that would allow me to start up the spreadsheet program and enter my actions and target dates that would eventually end up on the grid, ready for me to print or view and keep me on track. This was a great productivity tool and I have never stopped looking for ways to apply technology, even if I need an outside resource, to help improve efficiency using better and faster organization techniques.

As I have said previously, even if you have what you consider to be a unique set of circumstances, search for something that already exists. I almost never create a document, spreadsheet or presentation from scratch anymore. I save time by starting with something similar that already has formatting, formulas and graphics I know I'll need. The more productive you are with tools and resources, the more time you can spend on the quality of the information you are creating or storing.

Journaling is another good way to capture what you learn during a process, and with the search capabilities of today's tools, it is much easier to summon the information you need quickly. One key to success here is to have a consistent method for recording in your journal. For example, don't refer to the company's online learning program as "Computer-Based Training" in one journal entry, then as "Online Courses" in another. You may eventually find what you're after, but consistency will certainly help you to be more productive when searching your resources. Capturing what you have learned and preserving it for future use may sound easy, but it takes a very thoughtful and disciplined approach to pull it off. The only way it will get easier is by doing it religiously, and working out the bugs as you go. Whether you are a relatively new manager or a seasoned veteran, just imagine how helpful it would be to have an indexed catalog of your own "intellectual capital." That level of organization can make you more productive as well as help increase the quality of your work. Spend some time defining a process that works for you and you'll be glad you did.

COMMUNICATION

Communication is the central principle in the *Managing With Respect* model because all other components are dependent on the successful dissemination of information to help ensure understanding and enthusiastic action. This is very well illustrated in the process of employee development and career planning. Great plans are often not executed because communication was not clear about the benefits to be achieved or the expectations of those involved.

I once had an employee who was not very eager to sit down with me to create an individual development plan. We finally met to define career aspirations and activities that would help him maintain and develop key skills, and that seemed to go fairly well. When we reconvened with a completed document listing those goals and action plans, the employee was much less than enthusiastic. I was a little surprised and disappointed so I asked the person to be honest with me about what he was feeling. He finally stated that he could care less about this development planning process and was just going along with it to appease me, "the manager." I have to admit that, at first, I was angry. I had worked with this person to define a meaningful and realistic plan that would help him in his current assignment and to prepare for even more opportunity in the future. He had participated, but now I knew that it was for the wrong reasons.

I reviewed this unfortunate set of circumstances with my manager and our assigned HR representative to get some feedback and guidance. I had never encountered a situation like this, but the HR team had visibility to a much broader employee population and had experienced similar incidents. To meet the objective of providing all employees access to job and career development activities, we had to document the outcome, but it didn't necessarily have to be a set of action plans. Instead, I documented the fact that the employee chose to not participate in the process at this time, and had him sign it to acknowledge his understanding. The door was always open if he changed his mind, and it was my responsibility to offer this activity again in 12 months, but this met my management obligation to the employee and the company.

Obviously, the initial communication I had with this employee was not good. But by executing the process honestly and working to involve the person, the truth eventually came out and now we could move on. As a manager, you often have to deal with personnel issues that seem to be "no-win" situations. Under such circumstances, you've got to ensure you don't take issues personally and let emotion rule your decision-making process. I know it can be frustrating, but even when you go out of your way to help people, sometimes you have to let them make their own decisions. You can't make anyone do anything, and you certainly can't protect them from themselves. So don't put the entire burden on your shoulders, just because you are the one in charge. Communication, just like respect, is a two-way street.

Well, now that we have that depressing story out of the way, let's talk about something a bit more positive regarding good advice for people who have aspirations of taking your job some day. A peer manager of mine once told me about a simple piece of career guidance he called "L.A.P." It stood for Look, Act and Perform, and he used the term with employees who had high hopes of moving into management. It was a simple yet powerful concept especially when working with people to define realistic and meaningful career goals.

For example, if a person has identified that they want to become a manager in the organization, yet they are usually dressed rather sloppily and appear unkempt, they are not "looking" like the position they aspire to. Likewise, if they are always late for work, telling off color jokes and critical of every management policy, they are not "acting" like a member of the management team. Finally, even if the person has portrayed themselves well from an outward appearance, and regularly demonstrates a mature and "management-like" demeanor, there must also be some substance there as defined in their actual job "performance." Communicating this simple principle took only a few minutes but it usually resulted in one of two changes by employees. They either realized they really didn't want to be a manager or, they began acting more like one. Either way, it was a good method of getting them to open their eyes to reality and do some introspection which made for much better career planning.

 PLAN YOUR WORK AND *WORK* YOUR PLAN

Chapter 7: Recognition

When it comes to recognizing and rewarding people for a good job, many managers believe this is one of the easiest and most fun tasks they can perform. I say, "Fun yes, easy no." In fact, every bit as much time and effort should be put into planning formal recognition as is put into preparing disciplinary action. Why? Because it is an extremely significant event that carries with it implications that affect the individual, the team and the organization. Remember the underlying foundation of respect and tiers of responsibility that must be considered? Recognizing employees may be one of the activities that illustrate this best. Whether it is formal or informal recognition, it needs to be genuine. Let's delve into the detail using the foundation and pillars of our model.

RESPECT

You might think that providing recognition is always a sign of respect. Awards, promotions, bonuses and even a pat on the back can be genuine indicators of respect. But in some instances, recognition is done with ulterior motives behind them or with flawed logic or thought processes. Ever know a manager that chose to give someone an award because they knew it would infuriate a competitive peer of theirs? Ever see an overly sensitive manager promote someone because they thought that person could use the money more than others? "Playing games" like this shows a lack of integrity and respect at just about every level. The best practice is to take a methodical and unbiased approach to the task of recognition first. Look objectively at input and feedback and test the soundness of your decision based on the facts. Next, consider the affect this recognition may have beyond the obvious environment. Anticipation of negative consequences may or may not be serious enough to change your mind, but your consideration of them is usually indicative of a healthy respect for people and business. There will come a time when someone questions your judgment, but at least you can rely on the consistency of your approach to support your decision.

KNOWLEDGE

If you don't know what a person has accomplished, you can't provide meaningful feedback and you certainly shouldn't be writing up an award nomination or recommendation for promotion. Knowledge of performance worthy of significant reward is not hard to come by and doesn't have to be observed first hand. But there are many, many pitfalls ahead if you don't do your homework to define the criteria you are using and execute an honest assessment that is comparable to what you have done in the past and observed or learned from other parts of your organization. You don't do anyone any good if you quickly throw together a justification for recognition that will not stand up to scrutiny. If your recommendation fails to pass muster, obviously the employee will not benefit, and it's also possible that *you* will lose some credibility in the process.

If you are in the habit of knowing what your employees are doing, it will be that much easier to know when extraordinary performance is achieved. Armed with this insight, you'll also be able to write it up in such a way that clearly distinguishes it as superior. This can be very powerful when competing for a small number of award dollars or limited promotional opportunities. Once you have done the leg work and feel comfortable that an employee's work is worthy of recognition, you've met your responsibility to yourself and the employee. In going forward with a well thought out recommendation and understanding of your organization's recognition policies, you demonstrate your respect for that higher tier of the business. Winning graciously shows your respect for others that competed for the reward. Losing graciously illustrates respect for your management's decision, but if you're smart, you will also add what you learned in this process to your ever-growing bank of knowledge for future use.

ORGANIZATION

As you might have guessed, it's pretty tough to quickly summon all information regarding employee performance, recognition policies, budgets, deadlines, etc., unless you are organized. The ability to put your hands on the right information when you need it is not only effective time management but it gives you that good feeling of being in control of your work instead of your time and work being controlled by others. I'm not saying that you won't have days where all your work is driven by unplanned requests and interruptions, but even they will be easier to deal with if you have a system of organizing and accessing the resources you require with minimal effort.

In my experience, recognition is most meaningful and powerful when it is based on fact. Whether you cite tangible or intangible benefits, the ability to substantiate your assessment is critical to the success of your campaign and also reflects on your personal capabilities and integrity as a manager or supervisor. Physically organizing your resources, whether they are desk files, computer files or electronic folders, will take time but is worthwhile in the long run. Organizing your thoughts is also important. Some of the most impressive managers I've met have had extraordinary ability to organize thoughts and access them at just the right time. This is more than just having "good memory" but that is where it starts.

Whether it comes naturally or you have to work on memorizing important facts, it is this mind-organizing task that is vital to success. People who can access data to support their position are much more likely to convince decision-makers to do it their way. On the other hand, you may have a great deal of information from the past that is not relevant and you certainly don't want to simply show off what a good memory you have. Organizing your thoughts includes the creation of meaningful links between data that may have been stored over weeks, months or even years. It starts with memorization but ends with logical and meaningful connection.

So, if you have a method that works for organizing information about recognition programs and you have a way to call up the individual's accomplishments that substantiate the award, now all you have to do is make sure you carve out the time needed to write it up. This is also a task that will usually take longer than you anticipate especially if you want to be sure to do a good job. Base the time you take to document recognition on the significance of the award. For example, if justifying the awarding of movie tickets to the "Employee of the Month," you can probably be brief and to the point with your write-up. When asserting that an employee has earned a significant monetary award or promotion, you will want to spend a great deal of time ensuring a high quality and detailed explanation. This is certainly needed if you are competing for dollars from the recognition budget or from a limited number of promotional opportunities. But don't forget that this documentation will also become a part of the person's personnel file and you really want to ensure anything that is logged in that file is of high caliber.

Finally, whenever possible, find other write-ups that have been successful. You are most likely not the first manager to have to document justification for a big award or promotion, so use your peers, manager and the HR department as resources. You never want to "plagiarize" but using old write-ups can provide structure and language that may be helpful. Remember that this kind of documentation is an opportunity to showcase an individual. Organizing your resources to help you produce the best possible description of their accomplishments shows a great deal of respect for both the recipient and the organization.

COMMUNICATION

As I stated at the very beginning of this book, even significant recognition can be done in such a way that the person doesn't necessarily "feel the love." Most people would be proud to have a big promotion or award announced to the team or to have it appear in the company newsletter. But in publicizing such recognition be sure not to inadvertently embarrass an employee as it will certainly detract from the positive experience. Injecting humor in a presentation can be very effective, but it must be done in a respectful way and with consideration for all who will be exposed to it. If you are recognizing someone publicly, take a little extra time and thought to ensure you are doing it in a considerate and genuine manner.

One of my favorite stories of recognition was actually with an employee in a normal annual job performance planning and evaluation cycle. At the start of the term I reviewed responsibilities as well as criteria that would be used to assess overall performance. This was a solid employee, relatively new to our department, but she confidently and professionally described her objective of achieving the highest overall performance rating and wanted to make sure we were in agreement as to how to accomplish this goal. Now, just about every employee wants to get the highest overall rating, but few are able to create a deliberate plan, execute the right steps, and proactively seek regular feedback to ensure they are "on-track." I had to admire the employee's approach but more than that, I had to define the responsibilities and expected results that would actually allow her to achieve her goal. The department had some straightforward targets so defining the highest level of attainment was fairly simple. Subjective factors are always more difficult to define, but extremely important to ensure fairness with the individual and equity across the department.

Over the next 12 months, we continued to monitor progress and checkpoint every quarter to stay in synch on both expectations and performance. At the end of the term, I collected as much data as possible to quantify all accomplishments. The results were outstanding. All objective measurements met or exceeded expectations in every category.

The subjective evaluation could probably be best described as not "what" was achieved, but "how" it was completed. For example, did the person simply focus on her own targets and neglect or ignore team members? Collaboration and information sharing is clearly a job responsibility, so you can't operate this way and get the highest overall rating. Another critical area is communication. If you hit all your targets, but in the process your lack of effective communication alienates and confuses people, you have failed to meet your responsibilities in that area.

After pulling it all together, it was clear to me that she had done it. The next hurdle was to see if my management would agree with and support this assessment. This is where your credibility as a manager is so important. I had a pretty good reputation and track record in this organization, but I still had to substantiate this appraisal, describing both the individual's accomplishments and how they compared to the employee's peers. Of course my manager also has to ensure equity across a larger population, so providing an honest yet strong assessment was needed to increase my chances of being successful.

As I'm sure you've guessed I wouldn't have highlighted this event if it didn't have a good ending. The assessment was approved and all that remained was delivering the news to the employee. Even though I think she strongly suspected she had made it, I did not detect arrogance or a feeling of entitlement on her part. This reinforced my perspective that she truly deserved the high praise she was about to receive. Needless to say she was delighted with the outcome of that year and so was I. She would reap the benefits of this significant accomplishment, but so would the entire department and higher level organization. This kind of outstanding performance can serve as a great example for others who strive for excellence. In fact, you better believe that this particular employee's next set of job responsibilities included training others in the department how to do what she had done that year.

Now here's a story about managing a recognition opportunity where there were a variety of factors at play.

I had only been leading this particular area for about four months when I learned of the requirement for a new critical position that would work out of my department. It just so happened that many of the qualified candidates were already on my team. The job carried with it a very crucial set of responsibilities and a promotional opportunity.

I had a solid five years of management experience with the company and was very familiar with personnel policies and practices regarding this kind of activity.

However, I was new to the department and still in the process of establishing my own credibility and value within this new group. I had already acquired a pretty good understanding of the people in my department including their current and past performance, skill sets and career aspirations. My management had provided me good information about the new job, the business rationale behind it and the expectations. I was also empowered by my management to select the most qualified candidate regardless of seniority, past performance ratings, etc. I really couldn't ask for anything more as a manager, but I knew I had to do this job right for the benefit of the individual, the department and the larger organization.

There were three people reporting to me that were viable candidates and it would have been easy to simply select one of them based on their years of experience. Based on what I knew about the organization, this probably would have been accepted, no feathers would be ruffled and a calm status quo would be achieved. However, I had been around long enough to know that if I proceeded this way, I might miss a great opportunity to create a much better situation for an individual employee, as well as help improve the perception of department contributions and create some good results for the organization as a whole. Moreover, I needed to conduct this activity in such a way that all candidates had an equitable shot at the job while maintaining my own objectivity.

I decided to conduct the job search like I was an outside contracting firm searching for the absolute best candidate to meet the needs of a key client. I posted the job opening to allow all company employees a chance to see it. I conducted formal interviews with every qualified candidate, including my own employees, despite the fact that I already had some insight into their suitability for the job. I wrote up my interview notes and selection criteria in detail, then reviewed it with my manager along with my recommendation.

I was certain I had selected the right person for the right reasons, but was also prepared for some hurt feelings and possibly some controversy among the team. The individual who won the job was pleasantly surprised because he had fully expected that one of the more senior employees would be selected. He took this vote of confidence and, combined with personal skills and commitment, went on to far exceed anyone's expectations in that job for many years. This was indeed a great story for the individual and yielded many benefits to the organization.

As I mentioned earlier, I was ready for some fallout, and it came when one of the candidates was actually upset enough to escalate the decision to higher level management. A review was conducted and you can never know how this will turn out because, after all, much of the process relies on subjective criteria and judgment which can always be a matter of perspective. In this case, the objective reviewer saw clearly that genuine respect for the individual candidates, the business and personnel processes of the company were executed with great care. This resulted in a consistent and fair procedure that was about as unbiased as possible under the circumstances. I was obviously happy with the results but not necessarily surprised and certainly not angry. Even the escalation was a normal business process, so there was no need to take it personally. People and processes are not perfect but if you execute with integrity, you give everyone and everything a legitimate chance to succeed.

Recognizing talent and leveraging it for greater collaboration will yield more results and can even have a positive influence on keeping good people around to continue your success. This leads us to our next topic – Retention of Top Employees.

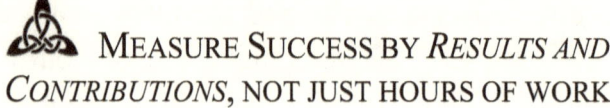 MEASURE SUCCESS BY *RESULTS AND CONTRIBUTIONS*, NOT JUST HOURS OF WORK

Chapter 8: Retention of Top Employees

Whether you are in a very competitive job market or not, once you have hired quality people, the investment you make in them almost always involves a significant amount of time and money. It only makes sense to continue to nurture this resource to maximize your investment and keep the people motivated. It's too easy to classify certain jobs and the skills required to fill them as "a dime a dozen." There are many jobs that require the same skill set but if you don't try to understand and encourage individual employees' uniqueness, you are missing a great opportunity to develop the person, and maybe even the job, into something that is better than what you started with. You owe it to yourself, the employee, and the company to maximize the value realized in the work relationship. Salary and stock options won't guarantee people stick around if you don't meet other, less tangible needs. Managers must know people well enough to ensure job assignments and other activities that are not only appropriate, but illustrate the company's understanding and even compassion for their current circumstances.

RESPECT

The new employee may feel a great deal of respect by virtue of the fact that they were selected for hire, have received a thorough and enthusiastic orientation and have been given the tools and direction needed to be successful in their job. Seasoned employees get to know an organization's personality or culture over time and if they like what they see and feel, you not only have less worries about keeping good people on your team, but this degree of satisfaction can help create exactly the kind of environment you want the new people to see. As with many other areas of management, retention of people is facilitated by use of the three competencies and we'll explore each below but first a brief description of a real-world occurrence.

A new summer intern had just started her assignment with my team. She was a bright and articulate young lady, excited and enthusiastic about this learning opportunity. I had provided her the usual department orientation and quickly got her working with an experienced member of the team. I knew that this particular employee was not the most outstanding performer or trainer on my team but certainly capable of showing someone the basics of the job. One day during the first week as I walked through the work area, I observed these two working as usual but noticed a very frustrated look on the face of the intern. I continued my stroll through the area to check on other workers but kept my eyes and ears tuned to that first workstation. Sure enough, I now heard an exasperated voice coming from the intern as she attempted to understand instructions and carry them out. I observed from a distance for a while and then made the decision to intervene. Without making a big deal I wandered over while the employee and intern stood together and asked, "How's it going?" The one word answers from both confirmed my suspicion that something was up. I then asked the intern if she had a minute to come to my office and checked to make sure my employee could do without her help for a little while.

We left the work area and I headed to the vending machines where I purchased a black coffee for me and a soft drink for the intern. In my office we sipped our beverages and I could see that she was slightly nervous and obviously wondering what the heck was going on. I told her that I simply thought she could use a little break from the work area and she started to break down, explaining why she had become so flustered. It only took a few minutes before she appeared calm and comfortable again, seemingly better for having had these few cathartic minutes. I took the opportunity to explain how there would be times when the job presented such challenges and not to be overly concerned. This was just a small bump in a long road and I honestly saw every indication that she was capable of success and learning with us this summer. A few minutes later she was back to work with renewed confidence.

Handling the situation this way allowed the intern time to compose herself and avoid a more public breakdown. It also provided some time for the employee to collect his thoughts and hopefully alter his training strategy. There was no need to "air dirty laundry" in a room full of colleagues, but it was necessary to intercede to ensure minimal disruption to the work environment and provide feedback to the people involved. You may not always be able to avoid addressing problems in an open forum but you can preserve the respect of participants better if you get out of the mainstream.

KNOWLEDGE

Good awareness of what is going on with individuals, your department, the organization and company as a whole gives you the ability to make better decisions. In fact, understanding the "big picture" can allow you to be more successful when justifying staffing levels. For example, the manager who knows the value of a person to the department may have a good argument to maintain the expertise that person brings to the team. But knowing how critical that person's skills are to the larger organization gives you an even more powerful business case to keep them around. And notice that I said "business case," not personnel. Retaining employees for a compelling personal reason is certainly valid, but you will be better off citing the business value first and then bolstering your case with the personnel discussion. Don't forget that as a manager, you have a responsibility to learn the skills and work performance of each person as well as understand your department's contribution to the larger organization. Employees, new and seasoned, are much more comfortable working for a manager "in the know." I don't care much for the political maneuvering or power struggles that go on in an organization, but to be effective as a manager, you really have to be aware of your environment and learn how to operate within it to produce meaningful results in line with expectations.

And for heaven's sake, don't forget to regularly tap into that tremendous database of knowledge found in the hearts and minds of your staff. Don't think that just because you are an experienced well-known manager in the organization that you don't have something to learn from the troops. Keep your ears open for facts regardless of the source, test them for reliability and sensibility, then turn it into the "intelligence" needed to maintain credibility for yourself and your team. I'm not suggesting that you perform unnatural acts to have people "think" you are a well-respected member of the organization, and therefore want to stay on your team. You have to stay true to your own principles, but when people see that this includes a real commitment to understanding your surroundings and ability to adapt to change using an intelligent approach, they will usually recognize the value of that "business maturity" and what it means to their longevity as well.

Having a thorough knowledge of company policies and practices and local programs is also an essential part of your intellectual capital when it comes to retaining skilled individuals. In the 21st century it is virtually impossible to know all aspects of all programs, but it is incumbent upon you to have at least a high level understanding as well as a process for getting answers to the questions of employees. Your ability to get answers that help people make more informed decisions illustrates your commitment to making employees successful. You also continue to build your own personal base of knowledge and over time, become a better resource to everyone, including yourself.

ORGANIZATION

No one really wants to work for a scatter brain. Having a reputation for being disorganized, even if it is just perception, can affect your credibility and hamper efforts to retain talented people. You must find methods for organizing your work and managing your time and allow people in your charge to see a solid role model. Modeling the behavior you expect from subordinates is a critical concept that can easily be overlooked by managers. Some managers overlook it intentionally, saying, "Do as I say, not as I do." They are in charge, so it is their right to operate that way. But most people don't need to be reminded who the boss is. They know you have the authority. It is much more helpful to address an issue with an employee if you can point to your own actions to illustrate what you expect. For example, you have a better chance of affecting positive change with an employee who is always late, if you have a good track record in that area yourself.

Maintaining a good understanding of what keeps your team members motivated takes some hard work, but it is well worth it. Taking advantage of available resources to help you keep high levels of enthusiasm requires information but you also have to be organized to bring the right resources to bear in a timely manner and to the right people and circumstances. Many managers get so busy with the business aspects of their job that the personnel work never becomes a priority. For example, the last thing you might want to do after a grueling 12 hour day or 80 hour week is take time to read the details of the new company "stock option program." It might even be on your "To Do" list or buried somewhere in your email inbox, but it just never quite gets to the top. So, you miss a deadline for submitting the names of qualified people in your department to compete for a limited number of stock option awards. I would much rather have a discussion with an employee about why they were not selected for the recognition than why they weren't even in the mix for consideration. There will always be more items on your list of things to do than you can ever get to. But when prioritizing that list, I suggest you give at least equal weight to the personnel action items as to the business ones.

COMMUNICATION

People appreciate a manager who communicates openly, honestly and frequently. When employees come to realize that you value regular and meaningful communication, they will worry less about missing something important and be able to focus on the things that can produce the results that will make them successful. In essence, you "have their backs" and they will recognize and appreciate it.

One communication method I have found to be effective is to read and analyze documents (printed or electronic versions) before "bucking" them to the team. Whether the item is just informational or something that requires action, if I am going to review the details anyway, I might as well provide my perspective and insight to everyone before sending it out. Some people like to take a quick glance and determine who to send it to just get it "off their desk" as quickly as possible. If your hurriedness results in misinterpretation and confusion, you have no one to blame but yourself.

Many people will appreciate the fact that you took the time to read and comment on the information so they may consider it along with their own review. You won't always have the luxury of doing this but if you don't have time, just be sure to let people know what you expect them to do with it. When you forward something with a simple "FYI (For Your Information)," don't expect to have any action taken or even get feedback on it. And, if action is required, state that succinctly such as, "Please review and provide brief feedback by end of the day Tuesday." This leaves little doubt that you expect something back regarding the note. Finally, you better have a follow-up method to ensure everyone hits the reply deadline. If you never follow up, even conscientious people tend to put a low priority on such items. Be prepared to "inspect" what you "expect" because this will illustrate that you respect your team members' time and expect the same in return.

In one of my management assignments, I arrived on the third day to find an envelope on my desk. To my surprise, it contained the resignation of one of my team members. I sought some insight from the former manager and learned that this was a solid employee but not necessarily enthralled with her current assignment. Reviewing her personnel file, I saw nothing but a good track record so I decided to meet with her and get a better understanding of the situation.

She shared with me that she felt out of place doing the job she had and thought a change was warranted. Her background included a variety of administrative assignments where she excelled and was well respected. Her current position involved more information technology and while it was an area that paid more than the admin roles, she just didn't have the enthusiasm and opportunity to excel that she did previously. Because I was new to my assignment, I had a great deal of administrative "set-up" to accomplish so I asked the employee if she would consider staying a while longer and I would utilize her talents to help me get organized in the new job. She agreed to do this and then revisit the situation in a month or so. As the weeks went on it was very apparent that her administrative skills were indeed outstanding. She completed her regular job assignments and spent extra hours helping me to document department procedures and build the disciplined structure that would eventually make us a successful team, able to sustain high levels of performance. Despite the fact that she was still doing her old job, her job satisfaction skyrocketed. She continued on with the department for many years and was still there when I left. I truly believe that both she and the organization were better off with her staying on board than if I had accepted her resignation.

This story is a winning situation on many levels. Without a good understanding (or *Knowledge*) of the circumstances, you cannot accomplish an accurate assessment of the impact caused by losing a person from your department. It takes time, information and a deliberate approach to analyze facts and intangible input that will be relevant to your evaluation (*Organization*). And, without some solid interpersonal skills and a well thought out plan, you won't be able to *Communicate* the benefits that might result from the action you're suggesting.

Finally, you really must possess a genuine respect for people and the business to even begin approaching this kind of sensitive situation. It would have been easy for me to accept this employee's resignation and move on. But delving deeper into the situation made sense from both a business and people management perspective, and you don't get many of those opportunities. It was worth the time to investigate and even if it hadn't worked out for the employee, at least she could have left knowing that both she and her employer had exhausted all avenues in the hopes of achieving mutual benefit.

On the other end of the spectrum is the employee that is struggling, either with job performance, attendance, or other significant issues. We'll explore some good practices in the next chapter.

 PASSION FOR THE BUSINESS AND *COMPASSION* FOR THE PEOPLE – USE A BLEND OF BOTH

Chapter 9: Managing Marginal Employees

If there is one management area that can truly benefit from a good understanding of the *Managing With Respect* model, it's this one. Managing marginal employees, regardless of the circumstances, demands a great deal of time and patience. It is an unfortunate truth that you may actually spend more time and effort on tasks associated with marginal employees than doing things for the best people on your team. These situations often create frustration and tension that no one enjoys, but if you stay focused on executing each task with objectivity and fairness you will at least have the satisfaction of knowing you did the best job for the employee and the organization. You have to work hard and smart to create an amiable solution if possible, but don't ever expect the process to be pleasant.

 SOMETIMES THE JOB IS DIFFICULT AND NOT FUN; THAT'S WHY THEY CALL IT *WORK*!

RESPECT

Yes, even individuals who are not in good standing with the company are worthy of respect. It is not respectful to hide problems from employees. It is not being a good friend to let an employee "off the hook" when they have deliberately failed to do what they agreed to do. It is not impossible to fire someone using a respectful and dignified approach. When faced with managing people out of the business, factor in what is best for both individual and business. Don't forget that managing with respect for people is also good business.

As a manager, your job is to "manage" both people and business resources to meet the expectations of the higher level organization. When a business resource is reduced or eliminated, you might be unhappy for a while, but then you get to work figuring out how you will manage without it. The more quickly you adapt to the new environment, the better you will be able to clearly identify changes that need to be made. By moving on, you are illustrating the "respect" you have for the business decision that has been made. You are now free to use all other resources (brain included) to make the best of the situation.

The same thing goes for respecting people when they are not operating at peak levels, but dealing with people resource issues is "a whole other ballgame." More than 30 years ago, in my first management assignment, my manager told me, "Remember, you never really know what people are going to do." I've managed lots of different people in a variety of settings since then and I like to think that I had very few surprises because of the way everyone was treated with respect. But the fact remains, "You never know…"

You don't do an employee any favors by not addressing a problem with them. And, you don't do yourself any favors by berating, attacking or taking an issue personally with an employee. Providing feedback to employees regarding poor performance or failure to meet certain conditions of employment may be uncomfortable but it is indeed a sign of respect. Nobody likes surprises, especially when they are related to your livelihood. As a manager you cannot afford to get caught up in the implications (e.g., family life, financial circumstances, etc.) faced by a marginal employee. But that doesn't mean you can't empathize with the person and do your best to help clarify how they can help themselves and what you are able to do for them.

Early in my first management assignment, I had an employee who had been promoted to a higher level job and was really struggling in his first six months. He was actually a co-worker of mine a few years earlier but as his supervisor it was now my job to deliver the job performance review which spelled out where he needed much improvement. The overall performance rating was marginal, the lowest you could get without being put on probation, and even though I knew it was fair, I dreaded having to deliver the news. In my session with the employee I reviewed the details and provided as many illustrations as possible to support the appraisal. I also made sure to recognize his efforts to ensure he understood that a great deal of what he needed to do involved developing better skills to deliver the required results. He had a positive attitude, but simply lacked the knowledge at that point to be able to achieve higher level performance.

When I completed my portion of the review, the first thing the employee said to me was, "Thank you." I did not expect that! Despite the news of the lowest overall performance rating, he was actually thanking me for providing the feedback that would help him to do better next time. I have done hundreds of performance reviews since then but none were as easy as that one. "Easy" because there was mutual respect and sincere discussion going on. I've used my same methodology for years but have delivered very positive performance reviews where the person became argumentative and even angry. Always conduct this activity with respect but never have expectations for how people will react.

KNOWLEDGE

When employees are having job performance issues, possessing a good understanding of the facts regarding job and circumstances is critically important to addressing the right problem at the right time and having a meaningful discussion with the person. You can't change your entire work schedule to hover over someone, but you better have a legitimate way to collect and validate your feedback and conclusions. If you already have a good set of processes for monitoring performance, don't change it. Let this process serve you as it has in the past and the consistency of it will bolster your claim that you are treating all employees with equity and fairness regardless of circumstances.

Wherever possible, you should look to find the "root cause" of an issue. Many times a decrease in performance or absenteeism is simply a manifestation of a much deeper issue. I'm certainly not advocating that you dive into a person's personal life but understanding what might be causing an issue can often help create a better approach and possibly a better outcome than you thought possible. Here again you owe it to all parties involved to be thorough and work with facts that allow for the most expedient yet accurate conclusion possible. Taking the emotion out of a situation will often clear the way for a better, more objective process. But taking emotion out of the equation doesn't mean you can't or shouldn't have compassion for the person having the difficulty.

Remember, your "tiers of responsibility" include the employee, yourself and the organization. Sometimes there just is no "win / win / win" situation. Addressing issues is best done with factual information, consistent execution and compassionate but not frantic demeanor. The more facts and true knowledge you have of a situation, the more credible and reliable resource you are to all of the stakeholders.

ORGANIZATION

Having a solid organization system that works for you is a valuable asset when dealing with issues associated with marginal employees. You don't want to be in the midst of terminating a person for conditions of employment and be unable to put your hands on the numerous letters and documented opportunities you provided the employee. Being well prepared will help you to illustrate fairness and fidelity despite a strenuous set of circumstances.

If a situation reaches the point where terminating the employee is required, be prepared for all logical approaches to fail. Many employees believe that, despite understanding the process of progressive discipline and clear documentation of consequences, they will never really be fired. When reality hits them, emotion often takes over and you can do nothing but listen with respect, then carry on to finish the process. This may sound and even feel somewhat cold, but you cannot protect people from themselves. Throughout the process your responsibility is to document and illustrate management's position to help the employee understand and comply. But you can't make the employee change their behavior; that's up to them.

If you don't take anything else away from this section, please take this bit of advice to heart: Document EVERYTHING. Contrary to popular belief, this is not just a way to cover your tracks. Whatever you document should be factual and objective. No matter how frustrated you get, never write anything you would be embarrassed or ashamed of. Despite the fact that this process can be emotionally taxing, you must remain calm and objective. Just like many other circumstances you encounter in life, controlling your emotions in a stressful situation will allow you to stay clear and focused on the objective. In the case of employee relations, objectives and procedures can be very complex, so staying composed and performing methodically will increase the effectiveness of the entire process. I can tell you from personal experience that dotting every "i" and crossing every "t" is important but at the conclusion of the process, there is rarely any feeling of satisfaction.

COMMUNICATION

Even the most effective communication does not ensure agreement. Many times, the best you can hope for is understanding. As I mentioned earlier, employees already know who has the authority, so when involved in matters of unacceptable performance or conditions of employment, agreement is not necessarily a goal. In fact, more often than not, employees will NOT agree with your assessment of circumstances. Early in the cycle of addressing issues, you might get agreement and that's good. Employees may not have realized the problem and your ability to communicate it quickly and clearly can result in positive changes that resolve it. But whether or not you have agreement, if the problems persist, you have to strive for understanding. The employee doesn't have to agree with the expectations for improvement but they do have to acknowledge that they understand them – that's your objective.

Listening is a key skill here for it enables more effective communication. You expect an employee to hear and understand your counseling, not necessarily agree with it. However, if you put the onus on yourself to be an equally good listener, you may just have more success and progress in discussions. A good technique to ensure someone knows you are really listening is to repeat back to them what you heard when they have finished making their point. This is often used in interviewing but can be equally effective in a more stressful situation as well. If the employee acknowledges that you have "heard" them, they are more likely to move forward in the discussion. If you have it wrong, they have an opportunity to clarify. This technique may diffuse a volatile situation but here again, agreement is not the goal. You are attempting to reach a common understanding which can serve as the basis for further fruitful discussion and hopefully, improvement. Without this, even the best laid plans can fall apart.

As a manager, it is your responsibility to handle the issues of marginal employees. The human resources or personnel department usually acts in an advisory capacity. The ultimate rights and responsibilities for hiring and firing belong to line management but if you fail to keep your HR team apprised of these situations, you will be abdicating one of your responsibilities to the organization. I have known lots of managers who are critical of the HR department because they felt no added value from this function. Regardless of your personal bias with that area, accurate and timely communication with HR is critical to the process of dealing with marginal employees. The ultimate decision belongs to line management, but your position will be fortified if you have the support of the HR team as well.

One way to garner the support of HR is to ensure timely, accurate and objective communication regarding the issue and the employee. Granted, this is HR's opportunity to see deeper into your operational procedures than you might like, but if you can turn to your documentation to illustrate fairness and thoroughness for an individual instance, you can help keep the focus on the issue and not on you as a manager. The HR department may not know the details of each job in the company so if you present the facts in an understandable fashion and without emotion or editorializing, they will be more likely to accept your findings and conclusions. You will have credibility when you demonstrate that you have managed from strength. In this situation, the strength came from your commitment to understanding the details of the circumstances, awareness of HR policies and practices, and consistent execution of communication sessions with the employee, documented objectively and ready for review as necessary by those with a need to know.

Here's one final note on communication. It applies for this chapter but also in many other management disciplines. Don't be "transparent." In other words, don't simply attribute responsibility for a decision to higher management. You may indeed be the recipient of great pressure from above, but it's you who must have the one-on-one meetings with the affected employee and you who must articulate the process and decisions being made. You may not agree with the tact taken by your management, but if you can't convince them otherwise, then you better make sure you understand the reasoning well enough to communicate to the employee. More often than not, transparency will anger everyone. The employee feels they wasted their time talking to you because you are really not the decision maker. There is a good chance that the problem you have been working on now becomes your manager's assignment. You lose credibility in your manager's eyes because you did not contain the situation as planned. Don't get me wrong, many employees will escalate a decision to your manager, but your transparency shouldn't be the trigger for that action.

I know how difficult NOT being transparent can be. In one of my assignments I had a team of experienced professionals, all very satisfactory employees. The word came down that our organization would be participating in a layoff program to reduce the number of employees across the United States. This was simply a staff reduction to reduce expense, and my department had to do its fair share. The good news is that we went through an extraordinarily detailed review process to ensure as much fairness as possible when identifying candidates for the resource action. The organization as a whole was doing fine and had good people so it wasn't a matter of simply taking the employees with the lowest performance rating or the least amount of seniority. My business unit had to contribute to the layoff but only with a relatively small number of people. This might sound good at a high level, but because there were so few people being laid off, it actually made the individuals leaving feel even worse.

As did all of my peer managers, I identified a person that might be considered for the layoff using the criteria and process we all agreed to. She was a twenty year veteran with a solid record, so I fought to keep her until the decision was finally made. She would be one of the handful of people in our organization receiving her notice.

I had all my selection criteria and layoff program documentation ready to go before meeting with the employee. When I explained what was happening to her, she was so shocked, she told me, "This must be a mistake." It was a very understandable reaction and I empathized with her but plowed on with the details of the program and what would happen next. Her surprise eventually turned to realization and then anger – also very understandable responses, in my estimation.

She would actually have a short period of time to find a position within the company but it had to be in a completely separate division. This would allow her to stay on with the company, just not in her current job. Initially, this fact provided little consolation. In subsequent meetings, the employee continued to protest the decision and I could do nothing but assure her that the program was necessary and that her selection was conducted in a fair and objective manner. I remained as calm and unemotional as possible but sometimes this "robot" demeanor will aggravate a person even more – I can't say I blame them.

Over the following weeks, I provided answers and any help needed but the employee was obviously still angry about the circumstances thrusted upon her. I didn't apologize for the decision but didn't overreact to her change in attitude either. She eventually found a job and was able to retain her salary and benefits, so I was happy for her. We always had a good working relationship but I think she left with some bitterness and felt I let her down. I don't know if she ever realized that she was the victim of a program much larger than just my department, but it doesn't really matter because I represented the management team and could not, in all good conscience, say that I had nothing to do with this decision. Sometimes, doing the right thing is no fun and gives you no satisfaction at all.

 RECOGNIZE AND MANAGE YOUR *TIERS OF RESPONSIBILITY*

Chapter 10: Diversity and Teaming

Now, you might be wondering why Diversity and Teaming appear together in the same chapter. It is not by accident. Several years ago, I drew a parallel between the dynamics of diversity from an equal employment opportunity perspective and from a team building view. Managing the diversity of today's workforce requires an understanding of legal implications, company policies and business needs. Compliance to the law is obviously mandatory, but creative thinking may also be used to design an environment where equal opportunity and effective teamwork are not mutually exclusive. In fact, principles used to help provide equal opportunity to jobs for people are easily transferrable to the process of selecting members for work teams to create well-rounded, high functioning units.

Diversity is a crucial factor in establishing high-performance teams. The rationale is that a team with diverse skills, knowledge and experience levels will produce better results than a homogenous team. People from different backgrounds, environments and cultures bring a variety of perspectives and expertise that help teams exploit diversity for creative problem solving, generating new ideas and innovation. Embracing diversity allows an organization to optimize benefits and business value using a deliberate approach to selecting the right match for the job or team.

RESPECT

Providing people a genuine opportunity to compete for a job they desire illustrates a healthy regard for them as people and professionals. To accomplish this on a regular basis, you should be able to discuss in detail your process and selection criteria for filling jobs and replacing team members. Job requirements and criteria may change, and you may even tweak the process periodically. But you illustrate respect for individual candidates, the organization and yourself when you can honestly say you execute your process with consistency and integrity, striving for fairness and objectivity in every instance. In fact, you owe it to yourself to have a process that is respected because it allows you to focus on picking the best person for the job, not on whether you will offend someone or violate a policy. To that end, consider getting feedback on your process from outside your department. Sure, you want your manager to understand how you operate and concur with your process, but your personnel representative should also be able to provide helpful input from an HR perspective. You don't necessarily have to implement anyone's ideas, but seeking the guidance of this area is a way to effectively utilize that resource and shows your respect for the expertise that exists there.

When you execute with consistency based on a respected process you have stability and therefore increase your chances of getting it right. Only time and trial will let you know just how effective your process has been but remember that business targets and objectives are not the only measure of success. Realistically, you must produce those business results, but don't forget to assess the effect you have had on the people. Increasing skills, broadening experience levels and creating higher degrees of job satisfaction can be powerful additions to an employee's repertoire. You must always be cognizant of project and business objectives, but with a process that recognizes diversity as a critical factor in the selection and management of teams of people, you will increase the likelihood that both individuals and the organization will benefit in the end.

Finally, remember that whether you are looking to provide equal opportunity from a human relations perspective or from a team building point of view, the procedures you choose to execute are not unique and separate "programs." They should be practices you have woven into the fabric of your operation. A respected process that provides equal opportunity for everyone makes both good business and people sense.

KNOWLEDGE

As you may know, there is no shortage of material to read on how to build effective teams. My suggestion is to start with some basic, well-known models and keep looking until you find one or a combination of components that suit you and your environment best. The terminology may change from one theory to the next but most agree that teams must go through phases or stages of development before they can achieve optimal levels of performance. Briefly described below, here are the five stages widely accepted by many business organizations:

1. *Formation* – a period when team members are getting to know each other and how they can work together to leverage skills and knowledge to produce results

2. *Contention* – a turbulent period where team members work out differences and define how to get along.

They begin to build on the familiarity of team resources and define strategies and tactical procedures. A code of conduct or set of guidelines for how team members communicate and interact is a key component of this phase

3. *Normalization* – as operations proceed, this is a period of stabilization for people interactions and operational processes. Team members work together to define what works and what doesn't, then revise and re-direct as needed to steady their environment

4. *Performance* – the ultimate goal of all teams is to reach this stage characterized by consistently high levels of performance over time by virtue of their people resource, meaningful procedures and exceptional execution

5. *Disband* – when projects are ending and the team is dispersing, there needs to be time to evaluate success and celebrate. If failure or project cancelation occurs, analysis of the details should be conducted quickly, then documented and archived for use in subsequent endeavors as appropriate

Recognizing the dynamics of team members and team maturation as well as trying to get the best possible business results can be a daunting task. Many managers or team leaders fall victim to the pressures of target dates and budget constraints, so the monitoring of individual and team development go by the wayside. Short term success may occur but whether you realize it or not, you may be sacrificing the future by neglecting the need to evaluate and nurture team performance.

Time is the precious commodity in this and many other endeavors. To maximize what you accomplish within this limited resource, commit to identifying what you know and what you need to learn to be successful for both short-term and long-term results. When it comes to managing business teams, you may already have good project management knowledge. This gives you the opportunity to learn more about teaming and then utilize that understanding to leverage the strengths of individuals and provide help where it will do the most good.

Knowledge of the individual team members and the team as a whole is needed if you are to create the synergistic effect that so many businesses seek. Diversity comes into play in several phases of a team's development. When creating a new team, you might think that choosing members that already share common skills, experiences, etc. will help you to get more done because there will be less time needed to get accustomed to each others' differences. This is true, to a certain extent, but it is short-term thinking. Diverse teams must learn how to work with each other quickly and this is a much more challenging environment. Challenging environments are where talented people are at their best. And when you, the knowledgeable team leader guide those efforts and recognize both individual and team accomplishments, you will realize more and better results faster than a homogeneous team.

Understanding the power of diversity in teams is never more useful than when you must select a new team member. Without a keen awareness of individual and team performance, you will not be able to define the criteria needed to replace someone or select a new member that complements, and ideally strengthens the team. Defining the needs of the team and selecting the right person is not a trivial task but it is a great opportunity to inject just the right amount of change necessary to move a team forward in terms of its maturation. Seek input from your team and define the selection criteria but stay open minded as you conduct the search. Don't let personal prejudices or biases get in the way of an effective decision. There are never any guarantees, but defining your criteria and taking a deliberate and disciplined approach will usually yield the best possible results.

Knowledge of the phases that teams go through and the ability to recognize them is critical to rewarding and celebrating at just the right time to have the maximum positive influence. Awareness of your own strengths and weaknesses is also a key ingredient to success and allows you to apply the right methods at the right time. There are many management styles that work but most people agree their best, most respected managers possessed and utilized a blend of styles. Here again, making the effort to learn some fundamentals about different management styles, and then doing some introspection will allow you to become a more self-aware, intelligent leader, worthy of respect in the eyes of many.

ORGANIZATION
Whether or not you agree with company, state or federal initiatives such as affirmative action, you must be aware of the law and reporting requirements levied on you.

Maintaining records and establishing a method for quick access will save you time and aggravation. Inconsistency is one of your worst enemies, so once you have defined processes that help you to meet all obligations, execute them religiously and be able to prove that you did. Audits often strike fear in the hearts of managers, regardless of the area being reviewed. However, good organization can help you be more prepared and have more credibility when participating in this process.

The tools available today to help keep every aspect of your operation organized are many. It doesn't matter what you select, but make sure you can stick to it, or find another way. I personally think spreadsheets are one of the most versatile tools you can utilize to quickly and simply manage all sorts of data related to business and personnel responsibilities. If you are more comfortable using a word processor or even a database software tool, that's great. These 21st century tools may have started by serving technical staff, but they have developed into extremely powerful management tools, packed with user-friendly functionality and even a level of intelligence based on how businesses and people work.

Leveraging these technology tools is a great way to increase your productivity and effectiveness as a manager or team leader. I have found many ways to utilize the standard functions of office software tools, including the calendar and task functions within many email systems to help me manage in a variety of work environments. Best of all, I rarely create anything from scratch anymore. When I have a requirement for a method and/or tool to serve a process, the first thing I do is look to colleagues and other resources to see what has already been created. There are extraordinary templates and other items available for free via the internet. You must be cautious when going outside your "trusted network" but the likelihood of finding something very close to what you need is greater every day. Just make sure to know your source.

So what's the bottom line? Planning and organizing all the activities of your business team is not a "necessary evil." Consistent execution of a defined set of processes using an effective set of tools is a methodology for excellence. The stability, reliability and auditability of such practices illustrate a commitment to efficiency and effectiveness. When coupled with definitive actions to develop the skills and knowledge of individuals as well as the maturation of the team, this environment will yield outstanding results and consistently high levels of performance. It is therefore incumbent upon you, as the leader, to ensure dependable execution and ongoing evaluation of performance using an organized, disciplined and intelligent approach.

COMMUNICATION

I can't express enough how important it is to be a thoughtful communicator. Sure, we all have put our foot in our mouth at some point, but if you commit to thinking about and practicing more effective verbal and written communications, you will get better at it and have a more positive influence. I've said it before but it's worth saying again, "Communication is hard work." In a team environment, consistency in communication is critical for success and it takes conscious effort and planning to make it happen. For example, ensuring you have a process for recording and distributing meeting minutes, and carrying out that process on a timely and consistent basis takes planning and resource. But think of the impact of not executing this simple task. Misunderstandings and misinterpretation of actions and decisions can affect project progress. Moreover, the lack of, or inconsistency of communication, can have a devastating effect on morale.

Even when you have taken extraordinary measures to plan and execute effective communication, you might not always achieve the results you desire. You must continue to follow up with people to ensure understanding and compliance. For example, communication of an important deadline or milestone that is months away will easily fall to the bottom of the priority list if not followed up on regularly to assess status. This is no different than monitoring a project budget for actual versus planned expense frequently to ensure you don't experience overrun or lose control.

When it comes to communication, perception is often reality. What I mean is that you must be aware of not only *what* you communicate, but *how* you have presented it and eventually, how it was understood and applied. Even clearly written documents can be interpreted differently by different people so you need to keep your eyes and ears open to ensure you address any deviation from what you intended. Finally, here is another pitfall to be aware of when communicating with people. Even when you know your audience, everyone runs the risk of being a "naïve offender." In other words, without realizing it, you communicate something in such a way that an individual or group considers it offensive. Sometimes you will be told about it (especially if you have the trust and confidence of the people). Other times, nothing will be said and if you don't have good awareness of your team members and the dynamics among them, collaboration and/or morale can deteriorate quickly. This phenomenon, albeit potentially damaging, can be overcome if you recognize the issue and address it openly without pre-conceived notions or premature evaluation. Just because you are the leader, doesn't mean you are always right. But even if you are "always right," remember that the goal is to ensure teamwork and help create an environment where all points of view are heard, considered and respected. I will restate my claim that there are many correlations between managing diversity and managing teams in a business setting. We would do well to recognize those times when the two converge.

IF THE TEAM FAILS, *YOU* ACCEPT RESPONSIBILITY. WHEN THE TEAM SUCCEEDS, GIVE *THEM* THE CREDIT

In the Customer Support Center environment I've mentioned previously, diversity of job experience was certainly a strength for the organization, both at the representative and management level. Because our charter included support for mainframe business applications, mid-range property management systems, two different point-of-sale vendor systems and a host of personal computers and software on both PC and Mac platforms, it was extremely helpful to have people who had actually worked in those different "end user" environments. As we reduced our staff, the individual's job performance and ability to raise their skill levels through education and training were primary criteria. But we also made sure to consider what kind of *team* we were building as we identified who had to be let go and who remained. In fact, although it was not one of our selection criteria, we did end up with several people who were bilingual, some Spanish and some French. In some customer support functions this would be a significant advantage and possibly a requirement based on who you were serving. If, for example, you serve large communities of both Spanish and French speaking customers, it makes sense to have a diverse set of second language speakers on your team, not just everyone speaking English and Spanish.

We also exploited the background of employees to help us write the most meaningful problem determination and resolution procedures. One of the best people to write or review your P.D. procedures is a person who has actually worked on the system before. This department was frequently scrutinized to see where and how we added value. So, tapping into the intellectual capital of a diverse set of skilled employees helped us to increase the number of problems we resolved on the first call and increase accuracy in reporting and first level P.D. activities.

At the management level, I worked with three other supervisors, only one of which was a long time company employee. All four of us were charged with pretty much the same responsibility but all brought different backgrounds and experience to the table. As part of the information technology organization, we all had some experience in that arena. But the blend of technical understanding and people management skills ranged from 5 to 25 years. That expertise along with a leader who knew how to leverage the best from each resulted in a team that worked.

Embracing diversity makes both good business and people management sense, so long as you approach it with open-mindedness, intelligence and respect.

 ONCE YOU HAVE DETERMINED YOUR STRATEGY,
IMPLEMENT WITH FIDELITY

Chapter 11: Harassment in the Workplace

Harassment is often a concern of management, but not necessarily because it is actually occurring on the job. More so the issue is that people don't have a clear understanding of what it is and what they are expected to do and not to do. In fact, incidents of harassment are often in a gray area, but if you make an honest effort to understand the issues, you have a better chance of keeping your work environment a happier and more productive and satisfying place to work. The last thing you want to do is ignore issues, treat an employee's complaint as frivolous, or jump to conclusions before doing any investigation. This chapter will discuss how to prepare for circumstances when offenders (naïve or otherwise) do not understand how to treat co-workers and others with regard to business relationships.

RESPECT

Ensuring a harassment-free workplace sounds like common sense because it is. However, that certainly doesn't mean it will be easy or that people in charge of work conditions are sufficiently trained to recognize and address issues to everyone's satisfaction. I think most people agree that employees do have the right to work in an environment free of harassment and management has a responsibility to provide that "safety." And once again, ensuring awareness of issues and addressing them quickly and completely makes both good people and business sense. It's in your best interest as a people manager to respect an employee's right to perform their job without unnecessary hassle. Your responsibility is not limited to simply ensuring they are doing their job. To really illustrate the respect you have for the individual and the organization, you must understand the environment, what contributes to it, and work to improve it wherever possible. If you ignore your surroundings and/or employee concerns, you are missing a great opportunity to improve morale and productivity – two critical factors for long term success.

You also need to be cognizant of your respect for the law regarding harassment. Most organizations don't expect you to become a legal expert but if you fail to comply with basic guidelines provided by your management or HR department, your commitment may come into question. By the same token, if you feel there is little or no guidance being provided, you have an obligation to request it. The same burden that compels you to proactively seek an effective anti-harassment policy and monitor compliance to it is also on your management. Too often, inadequate attention is given to creating a meaningful policy at an organizational level and each level of management points the finger at the other or at their personnel department. It may be fine to stick your head in the sand for a while, but when a real issue arises and you are not prepared, the problem can quickly grow out of control. Higher level management and the HR department may suffer some consequences, but it is you, the first line supervisor, and your team members that will shoulder the most significant burden.

Knowledgeable human resources staff working with line management should create brief, but complete policies that are easy to understand and implement. They may not be perfect but it is incumbent upon the organization to illustrate its commitment to understanding and addressing harassment in the workplace. It is also the obligation of every employee (management and non-management) to comply with those guidelines. Finally, you must indicate your ongoing commitment to a harassment free workplace by your actions. There are bound to be many occasions where you can remind employees about the company harassment policy. The off-color joke; the inappropriate comment about another's physical appearance; the inadvertent look or "rolling of eyes," can all be opportunities for you to illustrate your respect for the policy and the people.

 SOMETIMES *DOING NOTHING* IS THE RIGHT DECISION

KNOWLEDGE

Obviously the more you know about anti-harassment laws and your company's policies and procedures, the better resource you are for your employees, the organization and yourself. But you don't always have to be the one who knows it all. Even if you have a file full of excellent documentation on what to do when you identify an infraction of the harassment policy, it may well be an inconvenient time to start wading through it for help when an incident occurs. Before anything happens, line up your sources and strategy for action.

In my experience, having a knowledgeable HR department representative available at the other end of the phone was a great resource. This of course, would usually be your second call. The first one goes to your immediate manager to avoid the dreaded "blindside." Using HR is a smart way to go for two reasons.

First, because of their role in the organization, they should have more expertise and more experience dealing with such issues. They should be able to provide sound advice based on the most current laws and policies. Secondly, even if you could make a reasonable guess at what action to take, or consult with a peer manager on how to deal with the problem, using the HR representative for guidance and advice will most likely be looked on as the right decision if a review is conducted down the road. Now, you may think that this is just a ploy to cover your tracks, but remember, even though it may be a smart move, it is not the HR rep, but you (and your management) who are ultimately responsible for any decisions made and actions taken. With that in mind, seeking the resource with the most expertise and experience makes sense, regardless of what ultimately is concluded and decided.

ORGANIZATION

My best guess is that your information from the company training session on harassment is not at the top of the pile of documents you never use but won't throw away. That's okay. As discussed in the previous section, having a reliable source of information and an action plan you can invoke quickly, may be all the organizing you need. Any definitive method, along with your keen insight and awareness of the people in your charge and the workplace "climate" give you the tools you need to address a situation in a deliberate and intelligent manner. Remember that *what* you do is important, but being able to provide the *rationale* for what you did is equally significant.

Organizing your resources and approach will help you prevent panic. Weeding out the unnecessary information from company documents, emails, presentations, etc., will also help you to zero in on the most relevant data and apply it in a meaningful way to your area. If you're the kind of person who is very astute at analyzing your team members and the work environment, you might even be able to anticipate potential issues based on the demographic make-up, economic conditions, industry and jobs being performed. Whether or not you have this keen awareness or a sixth sense, use what you know to prepare for handling issues with consideration for the people in your department and the organization as a whole.

If you do run into issues, don't forget to document the facts, as you see them. This also takes some organization, but it is more a task of organizing your thoughts before committing them to paper or an email. Timely documentation will most likely be expected and that's okay because you really should record events as close to the time they happened as possible. But don't rush into a dissertation simply because you want to "get it over with." I understand the sentiment, but once you have published, you are stuck with the interpretations that follow. Take time to review events in your mind and then write down in a factual way what you observed, said and did. Leave emotion out unless it is critical to your explanation. Remember, you are not writing the next great American novel. The fact that your heart was racing and palms sweating during an incident is not relevant to your report. The fact that an employee became emotionally distraught and struck a co-worker might be!

COMMUNICATION

As important as your actions are, what and how you communicate verbally and in writing regarding harassment in the workplace can also lead to success or failure. If you make light of the topic during information sessions or in resolving incidents, you demonstrate a lack of seriousness that will absolutely undermine your ultimate goal of providing a work environment where people feel comfortable enough to produce results without fear. Do I really have to say that you should NEVER be the one to tell a dirty joke, ask an employee for a date, or voice your personal opinion on gay marriage? Unfortunately, even in the 21st century, I do.

Of course you are entitled to your opinions, but if those opinions disrupt the workplace, teamwork, or individuals, they add no value and shouldn't be used on the job. Let's be clear. There are absolutely occasions when your opinion about a topic is valuable to the people you manage. For example, it might be appropriate to have a very stern conversation with an employee about work ethic and better management of personal affairs as it applies to a lack of consistency or results on the job. It is NOT appropriate to render your assessment of the person's judgment or personal decisions outside the boundaries of their job.

You can be honest and helpful without being intrusive but this is indeed a slippery slope. Succinct communication directed at a specific issue that is clearly linked to job performance and expectations is your goal. Most people cannot provide such communication without a lot of thoughtful preparation, so make sure you know your own communication strengths and weaknesses before you go into a dialogue with employees. The midst of a heated conversation is not the time to try and come up with the right words. No matter how competent and confident you are, remember that you don't always have an answer to an employee's question. "I don't know," is a perfectly legitimate answer, especially if you are being honest.

Planning and practicing effective communication will absolutely help you avoid being misinterpreted and possibly labeled as uncaring, oblivious or worst of all, lacking the ability to provide the respect people are entitled to. So, wherever possible, don't leave these crucial communications to chance and don't avoid having the tough conversations. As I have stated before, communication is hard work. If it seems easy to you, you're probably doing it wrong. When you provide thoughtful communication to employees, they will usually recognize that you took the time to prepare and it will therefore have more significance and impact with them. And just as I have mentioned previously, listening is a critical communication skill that you should practice and develop.

I once attended an information session for employees on harassment in the workplace and saw a great example of how communication failures could easily lead to misunderstanding. During a group discussion one of the participants referred to herself as a person of color. Another person in the group was making a point and used the term "colored" during her response. The first woman heard this and was quite angry that someone would use such a term and let everyone know how inappropriate it was. But had she listened and observed a little more closely, she would have realized that the second woman was obviously very young and that English was not her first language. It certainly appeared to me that this was simply an error on her part and as it turned out, that was the case. The second woman immediately apologized and we all learned that she was unfamiliar with the term "person of color." She was actually trying to use a term that would not offend the first woman, but because she really wasn't acquainted with such phrases, simply put it in the words she believed to be right.

The two points to take away from this story are to listen and observe carefully before drawing conclusions and don't try to use terminology you are unfamiliar with. This is also an example of the naïve offender I talked about in the *Diversity and Teaming* chapter. Today, it would be difficult to find a workplace that does NOT have a diverse set of demographics. So, taking time to understand the individuals and make up of your organization is critical to having success in communication regarding harassment and just about everything else too. In the next chapter we'll discuss legal and ethical responsibilities, including the implications surrounding harassment in the workplace.

MANAGERS DON'T HAVE TO CONSTANTLY REMIND EMPLOYEES *WHO'S BOSS*, THEY ALREADY KNOW

Chapter 12: Legal Compliance and Ethical Behavior

This chapter is not intended to motivate you to become a legal expert. Rather, the reason for including it is to show how applying the *Managing With Respect* model can help you to have more effectiveness in your role as manager when it comes to complying with the law and dealing with ethical dilemmas. Being a first line supervisor is the most difficult of all management jobs. Effective management of people resources to produce business results is your main responsibility, so the more things you can get out of the way of achieving that, the better. That's not to say that the myriad of other responsibilities aren't important. Federal, state and local laws as well as company policies will often complement and support your primary work as a manager. But when your plate is full and you must decide what has to wait, understanding the affect on the people and business objectives should be a key element of your decision-making criteria.

RESPECT

A healthy respect for the law and the guiding policies and programs of the company is essential for smooth operations in any organization. If you consider such topics as labor relations, conflicts of interest and information confidentiality to be trivial and not relevant to your job, your employees will recognize that. Laissez-faire attitudes toward legal and ethical issues will most likely have an effect on your longevity in the management ranks too.

You don't have to agree with the law or company policy, but as a manager you must understand and enforce it. If you really cannot stomach what this involves, find another job. You must operate with fidelity to meet your obligations to employees, the organization and yourself. Often times, laws and policies begin with a reasonable or even commendable intention to protect workers and businesses alike. By the time they make it to your desk to implement, the positive nature of a statute may have lost it meaningfulness in the real world. If you can find the original intent of a policy, you just may be able to leverage its power in your environment. Or, you may just find a way to live with what you cannot change. Either way, it may be worth digging a little deeper to help ensure the stability of your department and team.

One of the ways you illustrate respect for the law is to ensure regular monitoring of compliance and follow-up on any actions identified as a part of your operational procedures. Many organizations only discuss the topics of legal and ethical obligations once a year at best. Some don't address it all until there is a problem. If you have a basic understanding of laws and policies that are relevant to your operation, work to integrate the most logical principles into your procedures. For example, discussing what constitutes a conflict of interest during the sales process before visiting a potential client is much better than only talking about it once a year when you have the annual "training" session on business ethics.

I've sat in many annual meetings that review the same topics every year and the most important questions I asked myself when leaving were not related to the law itself. Ask yourself these two questions. "Which of these topics is most likely to be a factor in my area of the business?" And, "How would I demonstrate my understanding and compliance if requested?" You can't possibly anticipate all scenarios or potential pitfalls, but with a basic understanding of how laws and policies apply to your operations, you can be prepared to weather any storm that comes your way.

KNOWLEDGE

Obviously, you can't comply with the law or company policies if you don't know what they are. And, just like outside of the job, "ignorance of the law is no excuse." As with many other management disciplines, the more depth and breadth of knowledge you possess, the better you will be able to discuss potential issues and address problems or just questions that arise. But unlike many other disciplines, legal and ethical compliance are fraught with gray areas so guidance on interpretation is essential. Seek out reliable information and sources BEFORE you need them. Here again, your HR representative might be a good starting point. Even if you have accumulated the knowledge and understanding needed to handle issues, make sure you have a conversation with your personnel department. You're not necessarily seeking their approval, but not asking for their feedback is a mistake.

Furthermore, as a first level manager, you probably have at least a few peers that face the same challenges as you do and you all report to the same person. Share what you learn with the team and ask for feedback and collaboration on more complex topics. In many environments, this kind of information sharing is encouraged. Of course, sometimes people resist and even hold back what they know because they feel that having more expertise will give them a leg up on others in a competitive world. This occurs all the time in businesses around the globe, but I propose that you don't fall victim to this kind of behavior because even if it does appear to breed success for someone, it is a short term gain.

In the "information age," sharing knowledge and collaborating on complicated topics is not just nice to have, it is imperative to an organization's survival. Moreover, the broader the base of knowledge and experience you build, the better. For instance, teaming up on creating a meaningful review of your company's code of ethics when dealing with customers would be good if developed by the team of customer support reps, but even better if you can extract some meaningful input from the sales team and legal department. More information and a variety of perspectives should help you to produce a most significant result that is not only relevant to people, but compels them to act when necessary. The only danger in this kind of activity is getting so broad and attempting to include so many people, that you never really accomplish your goal. Put reasonable limits on the scope of your task. You can aim at producing a comprehensive process, but make sure to establish an end date and stick to it.

Finally, keeping your knowledge current is also important when it comes to legal and ethical compliance issues. Having a reliable set of resources is wise and leveraging today's "information management" tools is equally valuable. More about this in the Organization section.

ORGANIZATION

Ensuring adherence to legal and ethical requirements begins with understanding, demands execution and ends with demonstrable compliance. You can't get from one point to the other without an accurate roadmap and that's where organization comes into play. Some companies do a good job of summarizing their expectations when it comes to ethical behavior. They may have defined a process for communicating the details and even have all employees confirm their understanding (or at least review of the policies) every year, in writing (or electronic signature). By all means, if your company has such a process, make sure you know what it is and what your role as manager is within that process.

In today's complex businesses, the legal and ethical requirements regarding intellectual property and other intangible assets is tough enough for lawyers to figure out sometimes so don't think you need to become the ultimate authority when asked questions by members of your team. In fact, many organizations train their management teams to not answer questions, but provide the name of a focal point in the personnel or legal department to ensure accuracy and consistency when responding to queries. If your company has things organized this way, count your blessings and follow the procedures.

To keep up to date on the most current requirements your company has for you as a manager, utilize the information channels established for you. In the 21st century there are also many ways to not only find information about any topic but stay current by engaging reliable service providers and processes. Today's tools such as RSS feeds, wikis, blogs and social networks can help to keep you up to date on changing laws, trends, etc. Look for ways to set up automatic notification of relevant info, and then you don't have to worry about proactively searching for the latest information all the time.

Above all, make sure you know the source of the information. Everyone browses the web looking for information and we usually start with our favorite search engine. But when the search results screen comes back, make sure you look at the source (company name, URL, etc.) before diving into the details. For example, if you seek reliable information about labor laws in your state, you are sure to get many opinions from web sites hosted by law firms, colleges and universities and even bloggers with too much time on their hands. These sites may have a great deal to offer but your best resource for the law in this case is going to be the official state or the *xxx.gov* site. And even when you think you have found some legitimate and reliable information, make sure you pass it by your legal and/or HR department before using it.

COMMUNICATION

Even if you don't agree with a particular law or policy, you must communicate to employees in a way that they will understand and take it seriously. There is an overwhelming tendency to be transparent when you have to describe rules that affect workers and you don't agree with them. In such cases, you should remain neutral and do the job expected of you. This can be extremely difficult but if you veer off into an editorial that results in the belief that you do not support company policy or the law, you will lose credibility and have a tough time addressing any issues that should arise. Remember, understanding and compliance does not necessarily equate to agreement. Your team will respect you more for supporting a policy you don't necessarily agree with than they will if you express your displeasure and contempt for established laws and policies every chance you get.

Communicating your perspective to your management is perfectly legitimate, especially when you can link a particular policy to a conflict with business priorities, productivity, customer relationships, etc. If you present your concern as a business case, you will have better listeners than if you just sound off about a policy you disagree with. In any event, the law or policy may have to stand, but raising the issue for review is better than not saying a word. How is it better, you ask? Maybe, it just provides some peace of mind, but maybe it also illustrates your understanding and commitment to the job and your determination to remove barriers preventing your team from producing results. It's a lot easier to face your team and your management when you know you have done your level best to identify and resolve conflicting policies and/or priorities regardless of the ultimate decision.

What and how you communicate to your team and individual employees is extremely important when talking about legal and ethical responsibilities. Let's say you just completed the most thorough and eloquent presentation of business conduct rules the organization has ever seen. As you stroll out of the conference room your assistant calls out, "Mr. Smith called to thank you for the gift basket." Your team knows that Mr. Smith is a potential new client and such gifts are contrary to company policy. You just lost all credibility regarding this ethical faux pas and may have even cost yourself much more in the area of respect. I know there are people who believe that the manager has a right to say, "Do as I say, not as I do." It may have its time and place, but I've never found this to be an effective management style when you are dealing with professionals that you want to keep engaged for long term results and satisfaction. In fact, if you do a good job of communicating meaningful information to your team and you actually "walk the talk," you just might have even more resource to keep an eye on things. When your team understands expectations well enough to help you monitor compliance, you know you have integrated these important aspects into your standard operating procedures, and it doesn't get any better than that.

Entire team understanding and commitment to compliance is equally important in our next chapter, Safety and Security Management.

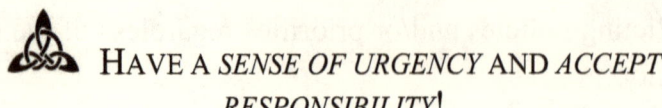 HAVE A *SENSE OF URGENCY* AND *ACCEPT RESPONSIBILITY*!

Chapter 13: Safety and Security Management

These two management areas on my list often get neglected. And the reason I put these two together is because I view the security of assets in much the same way as ensuring the safety of the people resource. In most large environments, the burden of providing a safe and secure work environment is handled by a specific unit of professionals who may or may not be employees of the company. Even though this makes good sense, as a manager of people, you should ensure your personal awareness of how and where the procedures of such departments intersect with yours. Regardless of other departments' responsibilities, as a manager you have every right to a certain level of awareness regarding the plans and activities that effect your operations and your employees. The safety and security of all business assets should be one of your concerns and obviously, none more important than the protection of your people.

RESPECT

When you practice effective safety and security procedures, you demonstrate your respect for the people in your charge, the organization you work for and yourself. In the information age, there are now almost an unlimited number of ways to get yourself in trouble so understanding the concepts of intellectual property and data as a company asset as well as the security measures that go along with them are critical for your continued effectiveness as a manager. Practices like sharing passwords and having no restrictions on access to databases can result in everything from an embarrassing moment to criminal prosecution. As a manager in the company, you not only have the responsibility to adhere to procedures, but the obligation to report infractions and suggest improvements.

Information asset security procedures often conflict with the productivity of workers. If you haven't experienced it already, some day you probably will run into a situation where your team is frustrated with their inability to do their job because security procedures create roadblocks at every turn. Security versus productivity, when it concerns the information asset, has become a classic struggle in today's businesses. Attempts to resolve such issues must be done with understanding and respect for both the security and business requirements. The end result may well be that the importance of one outweighs the other, but you must begin with an open mind and spirit of cooperation if you want the best resolution. Mutual respect for the people involved is a good way to get there.

Physical safety and security procedures and guidelines are often easy to become complacent about, but as a manager, you must remember to set the standard. For example, many people would feel awkward challenging a stranger that is attempting to enter their office building without "swiping" a valid ID badge (sometimes referred to as "tailgating"). It is everyone's responsibility to be alert for such violations, but if you let it go and one of your employees sees it, you run the risk of losing respect and credibility if you ever have to discuss the subject with them. It is also your job to help employees "learn" how to behave and what to do under such circumstances, especially if it is discomforting for them. Any training offered by your security and/or safety team should be taken seriously. It may not all apply, but be diligent about identifying what you and your team need to know. A serious incident is NOT the time to realize you don't know what to do or what to instruct people to do.

KNOWLEDGE

When it comes to safety regulations and procedures there can be significant differences and requirements based on the work environment you are in. Manufacturing operations will obviously have many more potential physical safety issues than will knowledge workers in an office. However, regardless of your environment, acquiring a firm foundation of knowledge of the safety and security procedures for your specific area is essential to providing the kind of workplace everyone wants and should have. Just as you depend on your personnel department as a resource for employee relations, so should you look to your security function for information, guidance and assistance with both questions and implementation of policy. You cannot become the expert in all areas so creating your pool of resources is critical to your success. And, as I have mentioned before, when you learn something, share it with others. You might be surprised at how appreciative people can be when you volunteer information that makes their job a little easier.

Something else that only you may add to the mix is an understanding of your people and any unique circumstances that need to be considered when implementing sensible procedures. If you have persons with disabilities for example, don't leave all the details of the emergency exit

127

routine to the safety department alone. Make sure you communicate special needs so the procedure covers everyone's needs. Common sense can go a long way when it comes to designing safety procedures that work. If you don't see the sense in a procedure you are being asked to implement, make sure you get clarification. Gaining an understanding of the original intent of a procedure will often allow you to support it or challenge it with more zeal as well as answer questions for your team.

Being knowledgeable of data and information as a business asset or as a privacy concern is an important dimension of your managerial responsibilities. In today's data-driven world no one person can possibly be an expert on all legal and ethical implications associated with the use and protection of information. So, my advice is to make sure you know what you don't know. In other words, if you work with customer data but don't know which components or combinations of fields are considered confidential or sensitive, you need to find out from the experts. If you work in healthcare and have heard about HIPAA (Health Information Portability and Accountability Act of 1996) but don't know how it affects your operations, make a plan to get help interpreting the law and implementing procedures that put you in compliance. Even if it is the responsibility of other departments to ensure your awareness of legal obligations and adherence to policy, it is you, not them that will have to answer the tough questions if a breach occurs. Be proactive and if you can't get the information you need, escalate for assistance.

Now, a quick word about audits. Auditors are often viewed as the bad guys. But whatever you think of the auditing process or people who execute it, you need to understand that their job is to find problems. Many people believe that if an audit comes up 100% clean, the auditors have failed to do their job properly. So, don't take it out on the auditor when they find an issue; that's what they are expected to do.

I was a manager in data centers for many years and was considered the owner of a variety of corporate system management and operational control processes during that time. Each year an internal audit was conducted and I was usually happy just to pass, even if there were some actionable findings. One year, my team had done an outstanding job of revising the process documentation and pulling together evidence of how our disciplined approach had improved since last year and could actually create the results it promised. We had worked hard to ensure the process met every single criterion for excellence provided to us before the audit. I was certain we would have a perfect review but it was not the case. A few minor issues were cited in the findings report, all very subjective and inconsequential to the overall effectiveness of the department. I couldn't argue that these were not valid criticisms, albeit insignificant.

When I met with the auditor he explained that he had never experienced a perfect audit because every area had room to improve. The audits were about meeting evaluation criteria but also about increasing effectiveness and building more and more mature processes over time. With that bit of

129

insight, I was able to let my team know that we had done an outstanding job and even though not perfect, our process was considered a center of excellence, a leader in the organization and positioned well to create even better results in the future.

You don't have to know it all to be successful at preserving and leveraging valuable assets. But you do have to make understanding how to protect them a part of your management regimen.

ORGANIZATION

Organizing your resources and reference information to allow quick and easy access to safety and security requirements can save you lots of time and headaches. Finding the time to do this is usually difficult but the investment you make will be well worth it. Over the years, I have built a list of contacts that not only includes people, but company names, web sites and other data that lets me find a resource quickly. Here again, building a useful resource will take time and thoughtful effort. But the tools of today can often make quick work of creating a contact that points you to an information resource long forgotten.

For example, most business people include a standard "closing" in their email notes so you can copy and paste that info into your new contact and don't have to key it in. Right clicking on an email address may give you the option to automatically create a new contact that includes at least the name and email ID, so you save a few minutes there as well. Phone numbers, web URL's, and physical addresses are good to include using the copy & paste function. I often add comments or notes to my contacts that either provide additional facts or point me elsewhere (e.g., a back-up contact name).

Even if you just work at your desktop computer and only have access at the office, all your contacts and related information are in one place and available with a few clicks of a mouse. If you have a smart mobile device, you can take all that information with you as well as revise and add anytime you need to. Searching for information is also facilitated by today's tools but you have to make sure to set up your data properly to take advantage of those capabilities. There is almost no limit to the number of contacts you can have, even on a relatively small mobile device so duplicating information is one way to make sure you find what you need quickly. In other words, you might have a contact for the person who is your information asset security officer as well as a contact called "IAS" which has a note with the name of that contact person. One or both of these contacts might have a website, hotline, even the name of a document you want to reference. Of course, all this information is only good if you use it. I refer to my contacts often and for the most part, can successfully use the information to get what I need. I have learned however, that no matter how diligent I try to be, there are times where I have neglected to create that new contact or update an old one at the time something changed. This method of organization works for me but I have to stay vigilant to ensure its usefulness.

Also discussed previously, if you are spending many hours organizing your resources and don't get the value, you are wasting precious time. It's like the debate about whether a messy desk is the sign of someone who is productive or non-productive. If the way you have chosen to organize information works for you, stick with it. If you sense that the task of organizing is exceeding the value you get from it, stop and revisit your objectives and methods. Most of my older contact records include a physical address but because I rarely ever need that information for people and companies I deal with today, I don't usually bother to take the time to copy and paste it into the contact record. Unless I know I'll need the address, I can use the company web site for that information and I know it will always be current even if they move. And this is just one less task I have to perform to maintain my own contact database.

Having emergency contacts and procedures readily available is extremely important because a real emergency is not the time to start thinking about what you need to do and where you can obtain help. I once had an employee who came to the office complaining about abdominal pain and dizziness. I let her rest for a while as she explained but it was obvious she was actually getting worse as we spoke. I have to admit feeling a little panicked because I had never encountered this at work before. But it was obvious she needed immediate medical attention and the bulletin board in the office had all the information I needed to call for help. Another manager heard some commotion and came in to offer assistance as well. He had been with the organization much longer than I and knew just what else should occur after the emergency call was completed. I learned a great deal that day, including that I wasn't as prepared as I needed to be for such an emergency. The next day, I began gathering all appropriate information for handling emergencies (medical, fire, bomb threats, etc.) and created my strategy for execution if ever needed. A wake up call like this can be a powerful motivator.

By the way, the employee was taken to the hospital and had emergency gall bladder surgery followed by a full recovery. I also have another rather incredible tale to tell from this experience but you will have to wait until the end of the book to hear it. Please, read on.

COMMUNICATION

If updates from your safety and security functions are communicated regularly, take advantage and revise your own procedures with any meaningful changes or new items. Keep in mind that you will also be briefing your team at some point, so the more succinct and relevant the changes; the more they will be embraced by others. Effective communication methods can often be used to remove obstacles that prevent the successful implementation of procedures that put you in compliance and may even enhance your operation. If it makes sense, you might even seek some review and feedback from your team *before* revising procedures. You don't want to have people feeling that they are doing your job for you, but if they have expertise that should be tapped, get them involved. It makes for better, more meaningful practices and can also create a feeling of ownership on the part of team members for consistent and effective implementation.

One of the biggest challenges you face is making communication of important topics interesting enough to be remembered. As important as they are, safety and security issues are usually not the primary responsibility of your employees. So, if you want to have a positive influence on their behavior regarding these topics, you need to present information in the most interesting and meaningful way possible.

People learn and retain information in a variety of ways so using a variety of methods will help increase your chances of reaching everyone. If you have a brief update, maybe a few charts with meaningful information will achieve your goal. But when more comprehensive presentation is needed, try to mix up the media. Using videos, acquired from your security department or found on the internet may be just the right item to spice up a dry subject and make it more memorable. Don't use anything that your company hasn't previewed and approved, but there are plenty of resources available for free if you do some digging.

I have also utilized free facilities for recording procedures and saving them in a library for subsequent use by the team. You can record your computer screen while you perform a process within an application and narrate as you go. This can be a resource that is a little more interesting and meaningful than a printed document. The free services won't usually have any kind of real security on them so be aware that what you put out there could be available to the world. But, used wisely, a resource like this will produce better results and possibly inject some fun into the workplace.

Above all, make sure you communicate serious subjects with sincerity and using a deliberate tone. The methods you employ for communicating may be fun, but the message must not be lost in frivolity. Just as you treat people with basic respect, so must you illustrate a genuine belief that safety and security procedures are in place to protect everyone.

 ESTABLISH A *SENSE OF OWNERSHIP*

Chapter 14: Managing Remote and Mobile Employees

RESPECT

Whether they work at home two miles from the main office or on the other side of the world, remote employees need to feel the same respect and attention you give to others that you see face to face each day. There are obviously many challenges associated with building teamwork when you have all or some of your employees working away from the office, but even if you have overcome many of the obstacles, don't forget that individuals need some TLC from time to time as well. It's very easy to let months slip away without contacting remote employees about anything but business topics. People differ in their perceptions and level of business maturity, so you should develop your ability to sense who needs a regular pat on the back and who would rather be left alone until the milestone is achieved. You must find time to do this or you run the risk of losing enthusiasm, collaboration or even a skilled resource totally.

In one of my assignments as a personnel manager for teams that supported information technology within a defined business area, I had people from a variety of locations in the U.S. This particular unit had a solid leader and many of his team worked out of the same building he occupied. In my regular discussions with the individual team members, I discovered that the most remote employee (two time zones away from the others) was actually feeling quite isolated despite the regular conference calls and occasional face-to-face team meetings he attended. In fact, he was contemplating leaving the company because he was uncertain about his ability to be recognized among his peers in this kind of work environment.

I had met with the team leader and knew that this employee had a solid track record and was well respected. My assessment was that the team leader was not only a good project manager but had strong interpersonal skills so I was pretty sure the employee's feeling of insecurity could be overcome. As is often the case today, travel budgets would not allow more face-to-face meetings so we put a plan in place to schedule monthly one-on-one conference calls as both a business and personnel status checkpoint. The calls were fairly informal and ranged in length from ten minutes to an hour. But the increased regularity of feedback and information exchange is just what was needed. The employee had many good thoughts that he now had a way to express without feeling awkward. The team leader was happy that the employee began to feel renewed enthusiasm but also delighted to get additional viewpoints and ideas that would help to improve business area planning and operations. By the way, this was a seasoned professional, not a new employee, so don't assume that only the newbie needs your feedback and attention to feel respected and valued.

KNOWLEDGE

As you may have noticed in the example above, having a keen knowledge and awareness of the people involved is extremely important when you try to assess a situation and take action that will be appropriate. In that example the solution involved knowing the people, the history, the current circumstances and the organization's constraints. When managing remotely, any "intelligence" you can gather to ensure a productive conversation is most helpful. In this case, I had never met the employee, but I learned as much as possible before and during our first call to ensure we had a trusting relationship. As his personnel manager, I would look pretty dull if I didn't have at least a basic understanding of his skills, education, job experience, performance ratings, formal recognition, etc. Knowledge can help facilitate respectful and productive communication that leads to a trusting relationship. Without trust, you will not convince people to take the leap of faith needed to overcome problems associated with working remotely; be they business or personal.

A knowledgeable manager will also be able to garner the confidence of their team members with more ease and more quickly than someone who appears less aware of the people's capabilities and the business climate. With remote employees, maintaining a strong understanding of their work environment, including the challenges that it brings, is essential to sustaining productive employees and teamwork. Many organizations have reduced expenses by having telecommuters work from a home office. Make sure you have all the facts about your company's policies for setting up needed facilities and equipment as well as reimbursement procedures so you can avoid surprises when expense reports are submitted. If you are not familiar with a work at home environment, you may need to find a good resource for other information about company policies and procedures so you can advise your people on how to be successful. The internet has tools that can often provide ways to have regular team conference and/or video calls for free. Become a resource to your team about these tools and you are helping to remove obstacles to productivity and job satisfaction that will raise your team's confidence level in you as an understanding advisor who cares about their ability to succeed.

If you work from home yourself, set the example for productivity and effectiveness, share meaningful information promptly and communicate expectations with the rationale behind them wherever possible. Look for opportunities to learn more about what works and what doesn't from other remote workers inside and outside your company. Be discriminating in your research (both content and source) but don't ignore the tons of information that exist via the internet to help you find better and better ways to operate. Most of all challenge your team to find and share relevant information about working remotely. Individuals may provide an excellent resource but in the right atmosphere, the synergy produced by many people contributing to the same set of goals can be astoundingly successful and rewarding for all.

ORGANIZATION

Organizing thoughts and materials before you pick up the phone or start up the video conference is paramount if you want to demonstrate how to be efficient when communicating with remote team members. Instant messaging and video conferencing tools can be effective methods of exchanging information quickly, but make sure you define some guidelines for all to follow. Based on usage, people can become frustrated and even suspicious that such a tool is being used for something other than just business communications. In many cases such suspicions are well founded as managers draw conclusions about time worked based on log in and out times, status indicators or other functions without ever defining expectations or procedures with employees. A clearly defined logical implementation of tools and procedures can be a tremendous productivity tool for remote workers. But beware of the pitfalls and make sure your people are polled regularly to get their input and feedback.

I once worked in support of a team of seven, all of us in the same building. We actually implemented the use of an instant messaging tool to allow quick communication of simple matters without having to walk down the hall or even pick up the phone. I created a document with access and setup procedures as well as guidelines for use. For example, we all agreed to be diligent about signing in as "available" each morning, setting the indicator for "away" when appropriate and signing out at the end of the day. Inevitably someone would be at lunch and forget to change their status on the instant messenger but no one overreacted and it worked well for the most part.

We also discussed circumstances regarding how to *not* use instant messaging. Urgent situations should be communicated by phone to ensure the quickest response, for example. Complex questions or issues that might take a long message to communicate should also be done by phone or in person wherever possible. We agreed to a "code of conduct" which said that we would not use the instant messaging tool as a way to discredit anyone or as a way to determine hours worked, commitment to the job, etc. This was a tool of convenience and productivity; not the primary communication tool, and certainly not a management tool for monitoring people or performance.

Less than six months later, I was relocating and would be working remotely from a home office. The organization and disciplined approach we practiced while in the same building proved to be invaluable as my transition to a remote support resource was about as seamless as possible. The team enjoyed being together in the same building but because we had gotten used to this process, our productivity didn't change and operations seemed about the same as before. The effectiveness of this tool and the trust shared by the team could not have occurred without a thoughtful and collaborative approach to setting it up. The code of conduct allowed everyone to have the same level of expectation and eliminated much of the fear associated with such a tool, so it could be utilized more effectively.

The more mobile workers become, the more you, as a manager, have to be able to measure results and not worry about where employees are and how many hours their putting in. If projects and other work objectives are clearly defined, you can measure actual performance versus planned targets. If a person's job is flexible enough to be done from anywhere (given the right tools), then you must be detailed in your description of expected results no matter where the work gets done. You also have to stay vigilant to ensure you are getting the best possible results from individuals and the team. Over time, people will become more proficient and therefore capable of more results in a given timeframe. If you don't know what your team members are capable of and don't communicate the expectations, especially as they change, you are doing employees and yourself a disservice. Organizing and even documenting expectations at a variety of experience levels will allow you to better explain expectations of higher level jobs and performance ratings which, in turn, will illustrate how this leads to more opportunity for your people. We'll talk more about communication in the final section of this chapter.

COMMUNICATION

As the central principle in the overall model, communication can certainly be viewed as a number one priority in just about any area of management. But managing remote and mobile employees brings with it a different set of challenges. You should strive to understand these implications because they will affect your business success as well as your team's perception of their job and standing within the organization. You must establish and sustain a trusting relationship to ensure ongoing productivity and collaboration. Effective communication methods can help you to do that. Lack of or inappropriate communication will do damage; sometimes irreparable, to work relationships, productivity, teamwork, etc. Staying on top of both business and people priorities is tough no matter what the working arrangements but if you don't have a thoughtful and deliberate plan for communication you are destined for trouble. And even when you have built and implemented a sound plan, if you don't go back regularly to make sure it's working, you're not going to get the desired results.

It's possible for employees who see their boss everyday to feel isolated and uninformed if there is no regular and meaningful interchange of information. So imagine how "in the dark" the remote employee might feel when communication is limited. Of course, even if you have set up a schedule of calls or video conferences to carve out a regular time for effective communication, you should also be looking for any non-verbal cues that issues or questions exist. Keeping your finger on the pulse of your operational "lifeblood" involves understanding your people resource and getting them to share openly about their work and career. Don't be afraid to be direct when having to communicate news that may not be received positively. Employees deserve to get the straight scoop in a professional and considerate way, just the same as you want to them to communicate with you.

Use the appropriate form of communication for the message to be conveyed. For example, personnel discussions dealing with job performance, salary, and career development should usually be conducted in person or by phone. Even though you could use email to advise a person that they will not be receiving a pay raise this year, it's much more professional and respectful to communicate such news where there can be a dialogue. If you need to present bad news by telephone and there is no time to schedule a call, make sure you know what you will say if you have to leave a voicemail for the person. Leaving the bad news as a voice message is just about as bad as using email. You want to illustrate your genuine concern by making the personal contact a priority, so if you must leave a message, make it urgent without sounding panicked and don't *hint* at the subject with clever language. "Theatrics" can diminish the professional and trusting nature of the manager-employee relationship, so give your communication careful thought before calling.

As I have indicated in many of the previous chapters, the effectiveness of your communication with individuals and the team as a whole can make or break your credibility and integrity. There is no guarantee that you won't encounter a problem even when you take time to plan thorough and professional communication with your team. But "shooting from the hip" is a much more risky proposition. Even people who are considered to be fast thinkers on their feet can quickly find one of those extremities firmly entrenched in their mouth if they don't take communication seriously.

 THERE IS NO SUBSTITUTE FOR *COMMON SENSE*

Chapter 15: Pulling it All Together

I set out to share my thoughts and experiences for management success by defining a simple model and describing ways to apply it in a variety of core areas of management responsibility. The model provides a framework which may be used as a point of reference for everything you do as a manager. It's not the only model that will help you produce success and stay on track, but it was built from the school of hard knocks, and is time-tested in a variety of environments and from different perspectives namely, large and small businesses; practitioner and consultant; line management and executive viewpoints.

The concepts presented and illustrated in this book can provide guidelines to help you navigate your way through the maze of complex business and people management encounters. But there are few easy or absolute answers when it comes to effective management in today's business world. Having a solid set of principles that you utilize without deviation will provide a sturdy and consistent approach that gets results and illustrates your strength as a manager. I encourage you to consider this information and use what is most meaningful and palatable for you. Be prepared to trust your model and revise it based on changing conditions and environments, but never compromise your personal integrity. Even when you find a decision you have made is wrong, if you arrived there using the best possible information and executed a thoughtful approach with consideration for all factions, you will maintain your integrity in this learning process.

Inevitably, you will be better at implementing and using some of the principles in the *Managing With Respect* model. For example, you might be meticulous about gathering reliable information and weeding out the garbage, then using it to bolster your bank of knowledge for effective operations. On the other hand, you struggle with effective communication, be it verbal, written or both. Spend more time strengthening the weakest skills and don't worry as much about the competencies where you know you are already proficient. In fact, once you have identified your strengths, use them to help you increase effectiveness with the others. If you are organized but feel inadequate when it comes to quality written communication, use your organization skills to create "best of breed" write-ups in a personal database that can be accessed and utilized quickly and easily whenever needed. If you possess excellent verbal communication skills but lack the depth of knowledge needed to do a thorough job of explaining a topic to your team, contact a subject matter expert and talk to them about helping you in an appropriate way. Even though the *Managing With Respect* model's components are few, don't fret over being more comfortable with one principle than another.

In addition to the model's components, the most important concepts to take away from this reading are that of *integrity, credibility* and *tiers of responsibility*. I have touched on all of them in the preceding chapters, but these concepts permeate all management endeavors and require active or proactive thought to help ensure success at both a personal and organizational level. You serve your employees and yourself well when you understand these concepts and execute with them in mind. Recognition of this awareness by others should come from your genuine commitment to excellence as illustrated by the way you actually do business day after day. Here is a personal example of how it can provide benefit.

While working at a large company, I transferred from one location to another. I completed a couple of assignments but after a while, I was assigned a department manager's job very similar to what I had been doing at my old location. Despite the fact that the two locations had similar departments and functions, my current job level was higher than its equivalent in my new location, but lower than the next step up. My management alerted me to the fact that a level change would have to be made (down a pay grade or up one) but they were able to wait six months before making the decision.

During those six months, the department had good improvement and success as we implemented a more disciplined structure for accountability of work product. Also during that time, the personnel teams at my former and present location discussed the discrepancy in job level and concluded that my new management could make the call on which way to move me. I was never in jeopardy of losing salary dollars, but being moved to the higher salary range would obviously provide opportunity for more money than the old level did.

Job and department performance over the six months was considered, but it was the transformation of department functions and operations, that allowed those accomplishments, which were the defining criterion for the job level to go up. I certainly benefitted personally but so would anyone taking over this job in the future. By planning changes for improvement and implementing with fidelity, my team and I had raised the level of expertise required to run this department and therefore, the department manager job level (no matter who the incumbent) would be higher. The organization reaped the rewards of a higher level function and the team received recognition for its contributions. This, in turn, opened up opportunities for promotion within the department because there was now a legitimate business need for higher skill levels in many areas. There was never an objective to define higher level responsibilities to drive promotion opportunities. But with a well thought out plan to improve and solid execution against that plan, it was obvious that the bar had been raised and in doing so, elevated the professional stature of many job positions in the department. Genuine commitment to business success through the intelligent efforts of people can yield even more success than you aim for.

Whether you are on the "fast-track" to an executive position or plan on leading the same department for 30 years, managers can get caught up in making quick decisions that may work for the short term but don't stand up to the test of time. Decisions that consider longer term affects and implications help managers to build a stronger future as well as addressing business needs of today. As much as I advocate that people be independent in their professional lives and career development, they still must be cognizant of the implications of their decisions on others even after they have moved on to other jobs or companies. This kind of integrity is what you covet because it will allow you to compete in a world marketplace no matter what the industry or job.

Now it's time to take the model for a test run yourself. But before you finish up, as promised, here's the other thing that happened during the emergency medical situation I cited in the *Safety and Security Management* chapter.

You may recall that I had an employee suffer a gall bladder attack at work and we summoned emergency medical services. They responded quickly but as we waited, another manager on the scene helped me out by advising appropriate staff on site, HR, my manager, etc. My manager was present just as the medical team was wheeling the employee out on a gurney. I had given him a brief but complete recap of events, but he obviously felt compelled to do something more than just observe. I followed as he chased down the EMT's wondering what he could be doing. He approached the gurney and told the employee, "Don't worry about work. In fact, why don't you just take the rest of the day off."

I'm not kidding. I couldn't have made up that story if I wanted to. I wasn't all that surprised that he lacked interpersonal skills, but this comment and timing was absolutely astounding. However, in keeping with the theory that you can learn something from every manager you work for, I proclaim this. As a manager, you may not always know what to do or say in a given situation. If you have time to determine something that will help, go for it. But if you're not sure, keep your mind and ears open but your mouth shut.

 YOU CAN LEARN SOMETHING FROM EVERYONE YOU WORK WITH, EVEN IF IT'S *WHAT NOT TO DO*

What Would You Do? (Part 2)

Finally, it's time to reveal the actions I took in the situation posed in the first chapter. Before reading on, I hope you have organized your thoughts about *what* needs to be done and *how* you will accomplish it. I provided minimal *intelligence* about the circumstances, so you may have had to create some assumptions before defining objectives and actions, but this is fine. As usual, I will present my description of the incident using the *Managing With Respect* model as the framework.

RESPECT – Since I already knew the employee, it would have been easy to jump to conclusions about the outlook as he returned to his old job and department team members. I wouldn't say that the decision to have him return was unexpected, but the fact that he was given a satisfactory, albeit marginal, performance evaluation did create one more hurdle for me as his supervisor. Any personal biases I had about the employee, his previous performance, the escalation, subsequent reassignment, and his return to my department had to be set aside. A "clean slate" included recognition and acceptance of all previous decisions made by this person, his management and any others involved at all levels of the organization. Nevertheless, there was also no reason for me to ignore my insight into this worker's circumstances. My objective was to treat him with the same respect as any other employee, but that doesn't mean I had to disregard my existing base of knowledge about this person's strengths and weaknesses. It was my job to provide an honest opportunity for him to succeed, and his job to execute.

KNOWLEDGE – One of my first tasks was to gather as much information as possible about the employee's year in his other assignment. I was looking to understand as much as possible from both employee and management perspectives so I could decide how to create a reasonable set of job expectations that would meet the needs of our department yet not set the person up to fail. Here again, you should not draw conclusions until you have completed your due diligence. The formal performance appraisal document and a phone conversation with the manager who wrote it provided a good overview. Unfortunately, the language used in the evaluation indicated *unsatisfactory* performance in many areas, and did not add up to an overall *satisfactory* rating from my view. But that was over and done with now. At least I had a better understanding of the employee's job performance during that timeframe.

The performance expectations for the job he was returning to had not changed very much but before I wrote up his new plan, I made sure to identify any conditions that might have changed his ability to perform the job again. I held a few initial meetings with the employee to re-orient him to the team. Listening to what people have to say about a conflict, even after it is over, gives them a chance to vent and hopefully move on. You don't have to agree with the person or even offer an opinion; just listen. If a situation is emotionally charged, the simple act of listening can often diffuse it.

ORGANIZATION – I created a detailed performance plan document that spelled out both objective and subjective performance criteria and expectations for the employee. To the degree that it was different than any other plan in the department, that's fine because it should reflect any unique business requirements that an individual is capable of performing. In this case, I designed the plan to take advantage of this employee's years of experience in the department. Now that he was re-joining the department, he needed to utilize his expertise and contribute to our success by leveraging his existing knowledge and utilizing current operating procedures to add value wherever possible. The performance plan and expectations document acted as the "contract" for this relationship. It is not a formal contract of any kind and it is certainly never intended to be an employment contract. But based on my knowledge, I expected there could be some controversy so I wanted to make sure there were no misunderstandings and we had a solid base from which to have discussions regarding job performance.

My next activity was to map out the strategy for regular monitoring of job performance. This would utilize my normal weekly and monthly reporting process for all team members with added reviews to ensure this employee was executing any new procedures as required since he was with the department over a year ago. I also created a template for quarterly job performance reviews that would serve as a way to provide meaningful feedback and direction as well as ensure documentation of my counseling and the employee's reaction. I made sure to schedule the reviews in advance with the employee and conduct them on time. Scheduling the meetings shows both a respect for people's time and a commitment to planned communications. It also gives employees a chance to prepare before the session, an activity that this particular employee actually took advantage of on several occasions.

COMMUNICATION – I was confident that I had provided the employee with a fresh start but as we approached the end of his first three months back, it was apparent that his performance was poor. It was reminiscent of earlier times but while that wasn't altogether surprising, it was disappointing that the employee had not taken advantage of the opportunity to bring up his level of performance. I am a big advocate of brief, informal feedback with all employees, so whenever I spotted something significantly good or bad, I would spend 30-60 seconds relating my observation. If you practice this regularly, you might find yourself remembering those times better when it comes to documenting overall performance. At times, I might even make a quick note on my calendar to ensure that when it came time to write a quarterly or annual evaluation, I was including activities that covered the entire period and not just the last few months.

During our first quarterly review meeting, I presented both objective statistics and subjective descriptions of performance to substantiate my conclusions. He was not argumentative and although I had empathy for his situation, I let him know that he had to do better. In subsequent counseling sessions, I was compelled to let him know that without improvement, he was headed for an unsatisfactory rating. As you might imagine, he disagreed, but even though I listened to his feedback with an open mind, he was not presenting anything that led me to believe I had misinterpreted his contributions or overall performance.

Open communication continued throughout the next nine months of the performance period but there was little change. When it came time for the formal annual appraisal, I drafted the document and sent it to my manager for review. I assigned an overall rating of unsatisfactory and even though my manager had been kept advised during this process, he wanted to discuss further to ensure fairness for this employee as well as across the larger organization. The result was a decision to move the overall rating up to satisfactory, but also to cite the major *unacceptable* areas as rationale for putting the employee on a six month "improvement plan." This was an action that could be taken only when approved by two levels of management and the concurrence of the personnel department. It was appropriate because it minimized the time that unsatisfactory performance would be tolerated, yet it provided the employee one more reasonable opportunity to respond positively to management counseling. I put the new plan in place and we began the six month performance period. As before, regular feedback included informal and formal sessions to ensure understanding.

As an aside, this kind of situation can be even more complicated if you also don't get along with an employee in non-performance related interactions. This was not the case here. In fact, this employee and I were very cordial toward each other when discussing the weather, family, outside interests, etc. It's understandable as a manager to not *enjoy* this process but you cannot treat people differently, like excluding someone from the holiday luncheon or avoiding eye contact when passing in the hallway. As difficult as it might be, you should always try to take the "high road" and not let personal biases intermingle with managerial responsibilities. This will only cloud the real issues and possibly reduce the credibility of your work.

CONCLUSION – As a manager, my objective was to provide the information, guidance and communication necessary for the employee to perform his assignment. My job was to give this person a genuine opportunity to succeed. You always hope that people will respond, but you cannot make them do anything, only keep providing honest direction and feedback. Whether they succeed or fail is up to them. In this case, the employee had obviously lost his desire to recognize the areas needing improvement and act upon it. His performance actually deteriorated and he was on his way to a formal unsatisfactory rating when a company retirement incentive program was announced. He had just enough years of service to qualify and even though he did not plan on actually retiring, he took advantage of the program and left the company.

I believe he saw the "handwriting on the wall" and this was a fortuitous way to avoid the embarrassment of being terminated. Either way, he was gone from the unit and although I was prepared to follow through on the process, this issue was now over. We'll never know if the employee would have tried to find a way to stay around a bit longer. But I do know that my department was a better team without the negativity he brought to work each day. I do believe that it was the right thing to do to offer him constant feedback and counseling regardless of how difficult and time-consuming it was. And I do feel confident that the outcome of this and many other difficult personnel issues can have a satisfactory conclusion when you *manage them with respect.*

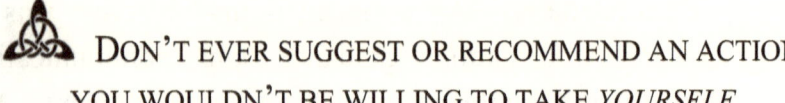 DON'T EVER SUGGEST OR RECOMMEND AN ACTION YOU WOULDN'T BE WILLING TO TAKE *YOURSELF*

Epilogue: You Take it From Here

As you read the preceding material, you may have made mental notes and had some extremely relevant thoughts that extended the concepts I included. That's exactly what I hoped would occur as you read because there is no way you could ever put all the great stuff you've learned in one short book. But if any of these chapters have provide a springboard for you to create, change or improve the way you view management responsibilities, I will be delighted. There are also two appendices that provide "laundry lists" of key concepts for success and my view of what leadership is. These lists are quick reminders of many of the concepts expanded upon in the book, and also represent what I consider to be some of the most important lessons I have learned.

For the business student and workers who aspire to a supervisory job, my advice is to read this book and all others with a discriminating eye. Without first-hand experience, you may not be able to identify with some of the illustrations presented but the model and concepts can still be used to help define a strategy you can apply to your personal set of circumstances.

For the new manager, use the model to complement the skills and abilities that earned you the job. If you haven't already, complete some introspection to make sure the model you implement is something you can live with and support regardless of the challenges associated with your environment. Prepare well for the job and all its complexity but don't forget that there will be failure. If you view failure as inevitable, but also as a learning experience, you will be much more likely to bounce back quickly and illustrate resilience to your employees and management.

For the experienced manager, use the model and concepts to reinforce your own practices or identify the need for change. Even if you have had a great deal of management success in the past, remain open to new ideas and integrate or reject them based on their merit or lack thereof, not simply tradition. One size does not fit all, and the experienced manager must learn how to adapt to change or run the risk of being left behind in the organization.

After more than thirty years of managing business and people resources, it's impossible to recall the thousands of decisions that led to success or failure. But in this writing, I have tried to extract the most meaningful ideas and concepts that have worked for me in a variety of environments and circumstances. My hope is that they will help the reader to avoid some mistakes but also to provide a resource that can be digested and utilized with relative speed. Today's world moves faster than ever so anything that can help you to get a head start can be valuable.

Finally, whether you agree with all or none of my conclusions and management philosophy, I hope this book has at least got you thinking about how we treat each other as people in today's workplace. Respectful management of people is, in fact, good business. In the world marketplace, differentiators can often be very subtle. Managing with intelligence, integrity and respect may not seem like subtleties, but they are certainly reflective of the honest and commendable objectives that we need to have if we are to thrive personally and professionally in the 21st century and beyond.

APPLY THE GOLDEN RULE: TREAT EMPLOYEES THE WAY *YOU* WANT TO BE TREATED AS AN EMPLOYEE

Appendix A: Words of Wisdom

1. Be smart enough to know what you *don't* know (Preface)

2. Better to aim at *perfection* and miss it, than aim at something less and hit it right on the head (Introduction)

3. Don't Forget *Long Term Planning* When working on Shorter Term Results (Chapter 1)

4. Communication is *hard work* (Chapter 2)

5. Develop *Business Maturity* (Chapter 3)

6. Identify, Manage and Close the *Gaps* (Chapter 4)

7. Conduct Regular Follow Up – *Inspect what you expect* (Chapter 5)

8. *Plan* your work and *work* your plan (Chapter 6)

9. Measure Success by *Results and Contributions* – not just hours of work (Chapter 7)

10. *Passion* for the business and *Compassion* for people – use a blend of both (Chapter 8)

11. Recognize and manage your multi-level *Tiers of Responsibilities* (Chapter 9)

12. Sometimes the job is difficult and not a lot of fun; that's why they call it *work*! (Chapter 9)

13. If the team fails, *you* accept responsibility. When the team succeeds, give *them* the credit (Chapter 10)

14. Once you have determined your strategy, *Implement with Fidelity* (Chapter 10)

15. Sometimes *doing nothing* is the right decision (Chapter 11)

16. Managers don't have to constantly remind employees *Who's Boss* – they already know (Chapter 12)

17. Have a *Sense of Urgency* and *Accept Responsibility*! (Chapter 12)

18. Establish a *Sense of Ownership* (Chapter 13)

19. There is no substitute for *common sense* (Chapter 14)

20. You can learn something from everyone you work with, even if it's *what not to do* (Chapter 15)

21. Don't ever suggest or recommend an action you wouldn't be willing to take *yourself* (Chapter 15)

22. Apply the golden rule: treat employees the way *you* want to be treated as an employee (Epilogue)

Appendix B: Leadership

Whether you desire to become an effective leader or identify those you would like to work for and learn from, the characteristics below can help keep you on target. I have encountered many managers in my career but few effective leaders. From my observations, leadership is . . .

1. Solving problems, not just identifying them for someone else to resolve
2. Seeking better ways to do things; not satisfied with the way things are
3. Taking action, not pointing fingers at dependencies and roadblocks
4. Removing beaurocracy, not just tolerating it
5. Embracing change, not just accepting it
6. Persistence despite resistance
7. Enthusiasm, not apathy
8. Passion, not passivity
9. Decisiveness, not wavering
10. Comprehensive, not "half-baked"
11. Consistent, not unreliable or unpredictable
12. Real commitment, not just lip-service
13. Real listening, not just "in one ear and out the other"
14. Personal commitment, not just looking to others to get it done
15. Providing vision, not just basic management direction
16. Exhibiting a positive attitude, not just wishing others would
17. Confidence but not arrogance
18. Ownership and accountability
19. Nurturing, not nagging

20. Open mindedness, not stuck in the muck of established norms

21. Using time wisely, not counting the minutes until "quitting time"

22. Taking people to "places" they haven't been before

23. A sense of urgency but not panic

24. Delivering the facts, be they good news or bad

25. Pride in every task

26. Working hard for what you want, not entitlement

Notes / Comments / Things to Do